Retrobates £2

Formula 1 98

Jean-François Galeron
The Grand Prix Season

Queen Anne Press
is a division of Lennard Associates Ltd
Mackerye End, Hapenden, Herts AL5 5DR

© 1998 Source Publishing Genève CH Suisse
English language edition © Lennard Associates Ltd

ISBN 1 85291 593 5

Editorial consultant: Simon Arron
Cover design: Didier Gonord
Page design: Dominique Gambier

Formula1 98
Jean-François Galeron
The Grand Prix Season

Teams / Drivers / Circuits / Statistics

Formula1 98
Foreword

Dear friends

I have fulfilled a dream by signing for Benetton. It is one of the very best teams in Formula One, with several world titles to its credit. And that takes some doing. From my point of view, the fact that the team has an Italian licence is also a big plus.

I am determined to have a good year in 1998. The Benetton B198 has already shown that it has great potential and I am confident that there are good times ahead.
This is a very important season for me. I now have plenty of Grand Prix experience under my belt and if everything goes to plan I hope to win a few races.

I am very happy teaming up with Alexander Wurz. He's a very straightforward guy and a great driver. We get on really well and we will work together to do the best job we can.
Despite the new regulations and the grooved tyres, I think the championship will be the usual fight between Ferrari, Williams, McLaren and Benetton.

The original tests we did with these strange tyres did not go terribly well but I've got used to them now and I'm enjoying my driving. The driver has a greater part to play with the new rules though it will still be the best teams who continue to win.
That said, I think that the 1998 season will be exciting and closely fought.
My personal target is to try and finish in the top five of the championship.

I am honoured to have been asked to write the Foreword to Jean-François Galeron's book, which will turn all enthusiasts into F1 experts and give them an insight into the fascinating world of Grand Prix racing.

Have a great season.
With best wishes,

Giancarlo Fisichella

1998 Calendar

march 8
Australian Grand Prix (Melbourne)

march 29
Brazilian Grand Prix (Interlagos)

april 12
Argentinian Grand Prix (Buenos Aires)

april 25
San Marino Grand Prix (Imola)

may 10
Spanish Grand Prix (Barcelona)

may 24
Monaco Grand Prix (Monte Carlo)

june 7
Canadian Grand Prix (Montreal)

june 28
French Grand Prix (Magny-Cours)

july 12
British Grand Prix (Silverstone)

july 26
Austrian Grand Prix (A1-Ring)

august 2
German Grand Prix (Hockenheim)

august 16
Hungarian Grand Prix (Budapest)

august 24
Belgian Grand Prix (Spa-Francorchamps)

september 13
Italian Grand Prix (Monza)

september 27
Luxembourg Grand Prix (Nürburgring)

november 1
Japanese Grand Prix (Suzuka)

Foreword	4 - 5

Teams and Drivers 10 - 91

Williams 12 - 19
Jacques Villeneuve 16 - 17
Heinz-Harald Frentzen 18 - 19

Ferrari 20 - 27
Michael Schumacher 24 - 25
Eddie Irvine 26 - 27

Benetton 28 - 35
Giancarlo Fisichella 32 - 33
Alexander Wurz 34 - 35

McLaren 36 - 43
David Coulthard 40 - 41
Mika Hakkinen 42 - 43

Jordan 44 - 51
Damon Hill 48 - 49
Ralf Schumacher 50 - 51

Prost 52 - 59
Olivier Panis 56 - 57
Jarno Trulli 58 - 59

Sauber 60 - 67
Jean Alesi 64 - 65
Johnny Herbert 66 - 67

Arrows 68 - 73
Pedro Diniz 70 - 71
Mika Salo 72 - 73

Stewart 74 - 79
Rubens Barrichello 76 - 77
Jan Magnussen 78 - 79

Tyrrell 80 - 85
Ricardo Rosset 82 - 83
Toranosuke Takagi 84 - 85

Minardi 86 - 91
Shinji Nakano 88 - 89
Esteban Tuero 90 - 91

Contents

From the paddock — 92-111

Gerhard Berger, the last of the old school	94 - 95
Ken Tyrrell bows out	96 - 97
Grand Prix racing in the year 2000	98 - 99
A Formula One steering wheel	100 - 101
Postcards	102 - 103
The girls of Formula One	104 - 105
Infra-red magic	106 - 107
Whatever happened to?	108 - 111

Grands Prix — 112 - 129

The changes for 1998	130 - 131
F1 facts and figures	132 - 133
The cost of Formula One	134 - 135

Statistics — 136 - 143

Entry list 1998

1. J. Villeneuve (Canada)
Williams FW20 Mecachrome Goodyear
2. H.H. Frentzen (Germany)
Williams FW20 Mecachrome Goodyear
3. M. Schumacher (Germany)
Ferrari F300 Goodyear
4. E. Irvine (Great Britain)
Ferrari F300 Goodyear
5. G. Fisichella (Italy)
Benetton B198 Mecachrome Goodyear
6. A. Wurz (Austria)
Benetton B198 Mecachrome Goodyear
7. D. Coulthard (Great Britain)
McLaren MP4-13 Mercedes Bridgestone
8. M. Hakkinen (Finland)
McLaren MP4-13 Mercedes Bridgestone
9. D. Hill (Great Britain)
Jordan 198 Mugen-Honda Goodyear
10. R. Schumacher (Germany)
Jordan 198 Mugen-Honda Goodyear
11. O. Panis (France)
Prost AP01 Peugeot Bridgestone
12. J. Trulli (Italy)
Prost AP01 Peugeot Bridgestone
14 J. Alesi (France)
Sauber C17 Petronas Goodyear
15. J. Herbert (Great Britain)
Sauber C17 Petronas Goodyear
16. P. Diniz (Brazil)
TWR Arrows FA19 Arrows Bridgestone
17. M. Salo (Finland)
TWR Arrows FA19 Arrows Bridgestone
18. R. Barrichello (Brazil)
Stewart SF2 Ford Zetec-R Bridgestone
19. J. Magnussen (Denmark)
Stewart SF2 Ford Zetec-R Bridgestone
20. R. Rosset (Brazil)
BAR-Tyrrell 026 Ford Zetec-R Goodyear
21. T. Takagi (Japan)
BAR-Tyrrell 026 Ford Zetec-R Goodyear
22. S. Nakano (Japan)
Minardi M198 Ford Zetec-R Bridgestone
23. E. Tuero (Argentina)
Minardi M198 Ford Zetec-R Bridgestone

Teams and Drivers

■ **PLUS POINTS:**

- Excellent budget
- The coolness of Villeneuve
- Frentzen more confident
- Success breeds success
- Lots of testing under the new rules from the middle of last season

■ **MINUS POINTS:**

- Will Mecachrome keep pace with engine development?
- The departure of chief engineer Adrian Newey
- Official withdrawal of Renault

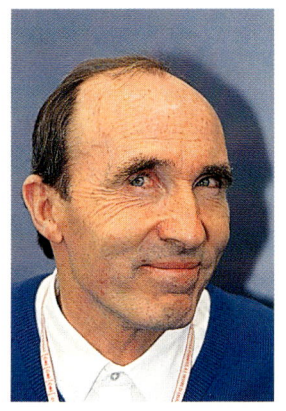

Managing director:
Frank Williams

Technical director:
Patrick Head

Address: Williams Grand Prix Engineering Ltd
Grove, Wantage, OX12 ODQ, Great Britain
Tel: 00 44 1235 77 77 00
Fax: 00 44 1235 76 47 05
Internet: www.icnsportsweb.com
Size of workforce: 260
First GP: Argentina 1975 (previous cars entered as Politoys and Iso Marlboro)
Number of Grands Prix: 379
Number of wins: 103
Number of pole positions: 108
Number of points scored: 1909.5
World constructors' titles: 9 (1980-81-86-87-92-93-94-96-97)
World drivers' titles: 7 (Jones 1980, Rosberg 1982, Piquet 1986, Mansell 1992, Prost 1993, D. Hill 1996, J. Villeneuve 1997)
Test drivers: Juan Pablo Montoya (Colombia) and Max Wilson (Brazil)

1997 result: 1st (123 points)

MECACHROME
Williams

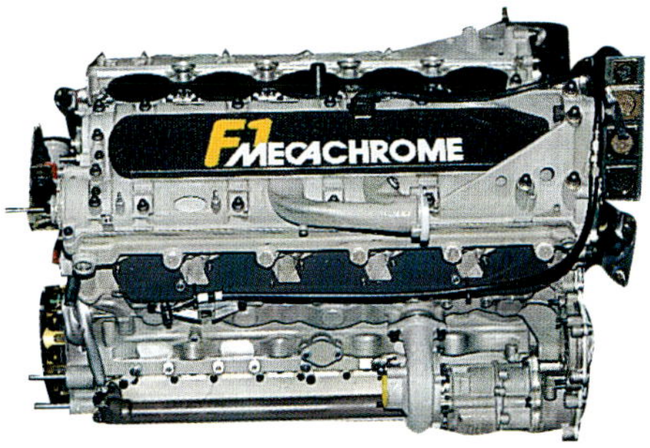

Mecachrome GC37-01
Number of cylinders:
10 in 71deg vee
Capacity: 2999 cc
Power: 760 bhp
Weight: 121 kilos

Williams FW20 - Tyres Goodyear

Perhaps the days of **Williams's imperious Formula One reign** really are numbered. After last year's feisty challenge from Ferrari, **the return to form of McLaren** will be a major cause of concern for the reigning world champion team. If **Jacques Villeneuve** is more motivated than ever before, and if **Heinz-Harald Frentzen** can at last fit in with the team's working methods, the Mecachrome (né Renault) powered Williams FW20 might be enough to haul the team out of a tricky spot and on towards fresh success.
Frank Williams rules his team with a rod of iron and both he and **Patrick Head** are relying on continued F1 supremacy. But the opposition is stirring and henceforth the bravura of **the lion-hearted Villeneuve** might not be enough to guarantee their objectives.

Winfield
VELTINS
GOODYEAR
KOMATSU
Winfield
Villeneuve
auto motor sport

One year to learn, one more to capture the world championship title. Usually this approach works lower down the motor-sport ladder - but not in IndyCar racing or Formula One. Yet Jacques Villeneuve succeeded. Narrowly beaten by Damon Hill in 1996, he gained his revenge last year after the infamous coming together with his arch-rival Schumacher at Jerez. A champion needs good fortune and the Canadian was certainly lucky on several occasions, but he fully deserved his title. Despite enormous pressure, he kept his cool. He is as formidable a fighter as his German rival, the only things which matter to him are the desire to attack, a good scrap and victory. If you win without danger, you win without glory. Unfortunately for Jacques, many races are won and lost through refuelling strategy. On-track overtaking manoeuvres, the true essence of the sport and one of the Canadian's specialities, are becoming rarer and rarer. In two years, Jacques has become the darling of the public. His atypical behaviour, his dress sense and his originality have all contributed to his popularity. When he arrived in Europe in the autumn of 1995, the motor-racing pundits insisted that it would be difficult for him to make a name for himself.
In two years he has become one of the few personalities to transcend the world of motor sport.
The Villeneuve legend lives on through the son of a famous father. He is in the process of writing a worthy page in the Formula One record books.

Team : **Williams - Mecachrome**

Name : **Jacques Villeneuve**

Number 1

Date and place of birth: 9 April 1971, St Jean-sur-Richelieu (Canada)
Nationality: Canadian
Place of residence: Monte Carlo
Marital status: Single
Height and weight: **1.71 m / 63 kg**
First GP: **Australian GP 1996 (Williams)**
World champion in 1997 (Williams)
32 GPs, 11 wins, 13 pole positions
In 1995, he won the IndyCar championship and the Indianapolis 500
Record in F1: **1996: Williams 78 points, 2nd in the championship**
1997: Williams 81 points, world champion

Personal car? **Renault Safrane bi-turbo quadra, a Renault Spyder, a Corvette and a '58 Chevy pick-up**
Dream car? **Dodge Viper**
Favourite racing car? **The 1994 Reynard Indycar**
Highlight of racing career? **Jerez 1997, of course, even more so when I saw Irvine wearing a helmet with the words 'Schumacher, World Champion 1997'**
Worst moment of racing career? **Halifax in Formula Atlantic and Phoenix in 1994 where my car broke in two**
Your favourite circuit? **Elkhart Lake**
Your least favourite circuit? **Detroit**
Your favourite driver of all time? **I don't have any heroes, but I admired Ayrton Senna a lot.**
Your favourite current driver? **Mika Salo and David Coulthard are good mates**
Favourite food? **Pasta**
Favourite drink? **Milk and root beer**
What sports do you take part in? **Alpine skiing, roller-blading and general fitness**
Favourite sports? **Alpine skiing and ice hockey**
Favourite sportsmen? **Downhill skiers are fabulous, particularly at Kitzbühel. As a general rule I like those who take risks**
Favourite type of film? **Action films and in particular *Pulp Fiction***
Favourite actor? **Val Kilmer, Christian Slater and Meg Ryan**
What do you watch on television? **Cable television and in particular MTV**
What is your favourite colour? **Blue, chestnut brown, green and black**
Favourite music? **Jewel and Smash Mouth**
Favourite books? **Science fiction books**
Your target in sport? **To win**
Beyond motor sport, who do you admire? **No one in particular**
If you were left on a desert island, what would you take with you? **A toothbrush**
What is the most important thing in life for you? **To protect my private life. I love to be myself**
What do you like most about your profession? **The danger, to be on a knife edge, to drive to the limit**
What don't you like about your profession? **I hate all the promotional work**
What are your principal strengths? **Sincerity and spontaneity. I like to be myself**
What are your faults? **I am egotistical and very disorganised**
Have you thought about your retirement? **First of all I've got to achieve what I set out to achieve. I'm only 26!**

Michael Schumacher feared the day when he saw his great rival climb behind the wheel of a competitive F1 car. He knows from previous experience in F3 and sports car racing that H-H.F. can be as quick as he is. The rivalry between the two men goes beyond the racing track. Schumacher's wife Corinna was formerly Heinz-Harald's girlfriend. When Frentzen's career lost direction and he sought solace in Japan, his compatriot was racking up success after success. Finally given a chance by Peter Sauber, Frentzen had completed just four races when Frank Williams offered him a chance to replace the late Ayrton Senna. Loyal to the man who had saved his career, he turned down this fantastic offer and only last year did he finally join the Williams team. Overwhelmed by bad luck, he found it difficult to acclimatise to life with the world championship-winning constructor. Despite a victory at Imola, it was only towards the end of the season that he started to show his true colours. He seldom got on terms with his team-mate Villeneuve. Now, well integrated into the team, he must stamp his authority at the front of the field. Are there going to be a few restless nights ahead for Michael Schumacher?

Team: **Williams - Mecachrome**

Name:
Heinz-Harald Frentzen

Number 2

Date and place of birth: **18 May 1967, Mönchengladbach (Germany)**
Nationality: German
Place of residence: Monte Carlo
Marital status: **Engaged to Tanja**
Height and weight: **1.74 m / 64.5 kg**
First GP: **Brazilian GP 1994 (Sauber)**
Best position in world championship: 2nd in 1997 (Williams)
64 GPs, 71 points, 1 win, 1 pole position
Formula Opel Lotus champion in 1988
Record in F1: **1994: Sauber 7 points, 13th in the championship 1995: Sauber 15 points, 9th 1996: Sauber 7 points, 12th 1997: Williams 42 points, 2nd**

Personal car? **Renault Safrane**
Dream car? **Mercedes 600**
Favourite racing car? **The Opel Lotus of 1988 and the Group C Sauber Mercedes**
Highlight of racing career? **My podium finish at Monza in 1995 and, of course, my win at Imola in 1997**
Worst moment of racing career? **The 1989 Macau F3 race. I was in the lead and I made a huge mistake! The 1997 season wasn't too good either!**
Your favourite circuit? **There is no perfect circuit**
Your least favourite circuit? **Imola**
Your favourite driver of all time? **Senna, Prost and Mansell**
Your favourite current driver? **Alesi when he goes on the attack!**
Favourite food? **Paella, prepared by my mother, fish and pasta**
Favourite drink? **Apple juice and mineral water**
What sports do you take part in? **Jogging, fitness and mountain biking**
Favourite sports? **Football, mountain biking and leisure sports**
Favourite sportsmen? **Christopher Columbus, that was a real challenge for its time, and I support Barcelona F.C.**
Favourite type of film? **A little of everything**
Favourite actors? **Jack Nicholson and Tom Hanks.**
What do you watch on television? **I don't watch it very often**
What is your favourite colour? **Blue**
Favourite music? **U2, Simple Minds, Phil Collins and rap music**
Favourite books? **German newspapers**
Your target in sport? **To be victorious in Formula One**
Beyond motor sport, who do you admire? **No one in particular**
If you were left on a desert island, what would you take with you? **A cook, my fiancée Tanja and some music**
What is the most important thing in life for you? **Health and optimism**
What do you like most about your profession? **I have always dreamed of having a motor behind my back**
What don't you like about your profession? **The self-interest of others**
What are your principal strengths? **To have well-formulated ideas**
What are your faults? **I find it difficult to change my mind**
Have you thought about your retirement? **No**

PLUS POINTS:

- A huge budget
- Ross Brawn and Rory Byrne in charge of the F300 design team
- All aspects of the F1 team back under one roof at Maranello
- The Ferrari engine
- The unquestionable value of Schumacher, who is in the mood for revenge

MINUS POINTS:

- Winning is now an obligation
- Irvine's inconsistent results

Sporting director:
Jean Todt

Technical director:
Ross Brawn

Address: Ferrari Spa
Via Ascari 55/57, 41 053 Maranello, Italy
Tel: 00 39 536 94 11 61
Fax: 00 39 536 94 64 88
Internet: www.ferrari.it
Size of workforce: 400
First GP: Monaco 1950
Number of Grands Prix: 587
Number of wins: 113
Number of pole positions: 121
Number of points scored: 2093.5
World constructors' titles: 8 (1961-64-75-76-77-79-82-83)
World drivers' titles: 9 (Ascari 1952-53, Fangio 1956, Hawthorn 1958, P. Hill 1962, Surtees 1964, Lauda 1975-77, Scheckter 1979)
Test driver: Luca Badoer (Italy)

1997 result: 2nd (102 points)

Ferrari F300 - Tyres: Goodyear

**Ferrari 047
Number of cylinders:
10 in 80deg vee
Capacity: 2998 cc
Power: 770 bhp
Weight: 130 kilos**

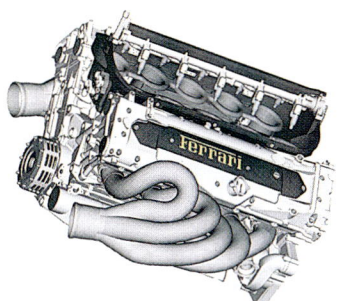

On 7 January 1998, during the official launch of the new **Ferrari F300** at Fiorano, company president **Luca di Montezemolo** made it plain that this is the year in which Ferrari must win the world title.
Last year they came so close ... No question, the Scuderia has everything it needs to accomplish its mission. And **Michael Schumacher** is out for revenge. The infrastructure, the operating budget and the technical team are certainly amongst the very best in Formula One.
This is a team which even has an aerodynamicist capable of taking photographs of the opposition while his own team is hiding away in **the heart of the Tuscan hills**.
Although it started off on the wrong foot, **Ferrari** remains one of the hot championship favourites. This year it is win or bust. Failure will be regarded as an absolute disaster in northern Italy, where there is presently a hitherto unparalleled will to win.

Don't talk to Michael about 26 October 1997. You'll risk ending the conversation before it has started. He has dismissed this notorious date from his mind. He has admitted his mistake and much has been written about it. One moment praised to the skies and idolised, the next he became a criminal, a leper. As he says today, he does not think that his reputation has been crushed. Public opinion does not judge a whole season on one race. Accompanied by his wife Corinna and young daughter Gina Maria, he spent the winter in Scandinavia revitalising his physical and mental health. He will return to the sport stronger than ever. For Ferrari, nothing less than victory will do. This is a challenge tailor-made for the German driver who is thirsting for revenge. And last year the title was not far from reach. However, if you were to ask him who was the best driver in the world, he would reply that Mr Villeneuve took the title, so he is the best for the moment. He knows that it is up to him and Ferrari to prove otherwise. If you talk only of the psychological battle between the two champions then already the pressure is mounting.
For his part, Villeneuve has said that Schumacher will never be a pal. Ferrari's quest for victory and the rehabilitation of Michael will be two of the main attractions of the 1998 season. His

formidable motivation, talent and indisputable racing genius should allow him to accomplish his mission. Some find it hard to like Schumacher, but you cannot dispute his racing nous, his flair or his will to win. If Formula One drivers were wine, he would be the champagne.

Team: **Ferrari**

Name: **Michael Schumacher**

Number 3

Date and place of birth: **3 January 1969, Hürth-Hermülheim (Germany)**
Nationality: German
Place of residence: Vufflens le Château (Switzerland)
Marital status: **Married to Corinna, daughter Gina Maria**
Height and weight: **1.74 m / 74.5 kg**
First GP: **Belgian GP 1991 (Jordan)**
102 GPs, 440 points, 27 wins, 17 pole positions
World champion in 1994 and 1995 (Benetton)
German Formula König champion in 1988
Record in F1: 1991: Jordan and Benetton 4 points, 12th in the championship,
1992: Benetton 53 points, 3rd, 1993: Benetton 52 points, 4th,
1994: Benetton 92 points, world champion, 1995: Benetton 102 points, world champion,
1996: Ferrari 49 points, 3rd, 1997: Ferrari (78 points, excluded from second place
in the championship after the crash at Jerez)

Personal car? **A Ferrari 550 Maranello, a Ferrari 355, a Fiat transporter to carry the kart and a Mercedes SL station wagon**
Dream car? **It doesn't exist yet!**
Favourite racing car? **The Benetton of 1994**
Highlight of racing career? **My first victory at Spa in 1992, those at Hockenheim, the Nürburgring and Aida in 1995 and standing on the podium at Monza in 1996**
Worst moment of racing career? **Imola 1994**
Your favourite circuit? **Spa**
Your least favourite circuit? **None**
Your favourite driver of all time? **Ayrton Senna, whom I admired more than anyone**
Your favourite current driver? **None**
Favourite food? **Italian food, particularly spaghetti dishes with tomato sauce**
Favourite drink? **Apple juice and fizzy water**
What sports do you take part in? **Karting, jogging, diving, cycling and mountain biking**
Favourite sports? **I like all sports**
Favourite sportsmen? **The cyclist Tony Rominger and endurance sportsmen like decathletes and triathletes**
Favourite type of film? **Action films and good comedies**
Favourite actor? **Tom Cruise.**
What do you watch on television? **News and good debates**
What is your favourite colour? **I don't really have a favourite**
Favourite music? **Rock and dance, and in particular Michael Jackson, Phil Collins, Tina Turner, Whitney Houston and Mariana Rosenberg.**
Favourite books? **Detective novels**
Your target in sport? **To win against strong opposition - and, as a result, to be world champion again**
Beyond motor sport, who do you admire? **Triathletes and the wife of Chancellor Köhl**
If you were left on a desert island, what would you take with you? **Corinna and my daughter Gina Maria**
What is the most important thing in life for you? **My family**
What do you like most about your profession? **To work with my team, to improve and to win**
What don't you like about your profession? **When someone tries to impede the work of the team**
What are your principal strengths? **I don't like to talk about them**
What are your faults? **That's for you to say!**
Have you thought about your retirement? **I think I'll always be somewhere around a motor racing circuit**

Like his team-mate Michael Schumacher, the frivolous Ulsterman is entering his third season with Ferrari. He fully accepts the status of his team leader, though he is keen to emerge from his shadow. Like a schoolboy at the start of term he is full of good intentions, and he is also very ambitious. This will be a very important year for him. He wants to finish second in the world championship behind Schumacher. In every race he wants to start on the front row so that he is regularly able to stake a claim for victory. If his German colleague should encounter any problems, then he will be there to pick up the pieces. In some ways Eddie Irvine is like a wound-up clock. Last season was a mixed affair for Irvine, with highs such as his excellent tactical drive at Suzuka and lows such as his crashes in Melbourne and Zeltweg.
He needs to find greater consistency to play the role of the perfect team-mate, just as Brundle did for Schumacher in 1992 at Benetton. If he fails, then he knows that his time with Ferrari could be up. On the other hand, if everything goes according to plan, he could become the main focus of Ferrari's attack should Schumacher move on to fresh pastures. Luca di Montezemolo and Jean Todt both consider this to be a make-or-break season for Ferrari. Hopefully, the pressure of his enormous task won't alter the livewire character, an unpredictable, anti-conformist man of mystery. This Dublin resident lives his life to the full,
and is well suited to the Italian way of life.
He always enjoys a beer and is invariably
in the company of attractive women. Formula One needs originality and diversity.
All too often uniform and sterilised, it needs characters who break the mould. In that respect, you can rely on Eddie.

Team : **Ferrari**

Name : **Eddie Irvine**

Number **4**

Date and place of birth: **10 November 1965, Newtownards (N. Ireland)**
Nationality: **British**
Places of residence: **Dublin (Ireland) and Bologna (Italy)**
Marital status: **Single**
Height and weight: **1.78 m / 75 kg**
First GP: **Japanese GP 1993 (Jordan)**
Best position in the world championship: **7th in 1997 (Ferrari)**
65 GPs, 52 points, 0 wins, 0 pole positions
Record in F1: **1993: Jordan 0 points, 1994: Jordan 6 points, 14th in the championship, 1995: Jordan 10 points, 12th, 1996: Ferrari 11 points, 10th, 1997: Ferrari 24 points, 7th**

Personal car? **Ferrari 355.**
Dream car? **None, because I don't own it!**
Favourite racing car? **The Toyota of Le Mans 1994**
Highlight of racing career? **My win at the Formula Ford Festival at Brands Hatch in 1997**
Worst moment of racing career? **The 1994 Brazilian Grand Prix**
Your favourite circuit? **Suzuka**
Your least favourite circuit? **Silverstone**
Your favourite driver of all time? **Senna**
Your favourite current driver? **Nobody at the moment**
Favourite food? **Chinese cooking and sausages with peas**
Favourite drink? **Miller beer**
What sports do you take part in? **Golf, jogging, ski boarding and swimming**
Favourite sports? **Golf and surfing**
Favourite sportsman? **Miguel Indurain**
Favourite type of film? **Comedies**
Favourite actor? **Liam Neeson**
What do you watch on television? **Comedies and documentaries**
What is your favourite colour? **Blue**
Favourite music? **Rock and Van Morrison, AC/DC, The Cranberries, U2 and Oasis**
Favourite books? **None!**
Your target in sport? **That a team will always need me**
Beyond motor sport, who do you admire? **Bob Geldof and his Live Aid Foundation**
If you were left on a desert island, what would you take with you? **A beautiful woman**
What is the most important thing in life for you? **To have fun**
What do you like most about your profession? **Living the life of a star!**
What don't you like about your profession? **The danger**
What are your principal strengths? **I have too many of them!**
What are your faults? **I don't have any!**
Have you thought about your retirement? **Yes, I'll go sailing and fishing**

■ **PLUS POINTS:**

- Two young but fast drivers
- Desire to return to winning ways
- The organisational skills of new MD David Richards
- Extra commitment from the Benetton family

■ **MINUS POINTS:**

- Will Mecachrome keep pace with engine development?
- Official withdrawal of Renault
- The relative inexperience of the two drivers
- A team lacking soul?
- Key engineers have departed without being replaced

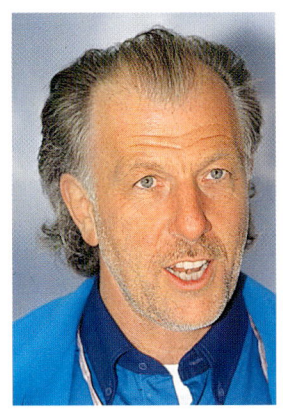

Managing director:
David Richards

Technical director:
Pat Symonds

Address: Benetton Formula Ltd
Whiteways Technical Centre, Enstone, Chipping Norton,
Oxon OX7 4EE, Great Britain
Tel: 00 44 1608 67 80 00
Fax: 00 44 1608 67 86 09
Internet: www.jnet.ad.jp
Size of workforce: 205
First GP: Italy 1981 (Toleman), Brazil 1986 (Benetton)
Number of Grands Prix: 251
Number of wins: 27
Number of pole positions: 15
Number of points scored: 798.5
World constructors' titles: 1 (1995)
World drivers' titles: 2 (Schumacher 1994-95)

1997 result: 3rd (67 points)

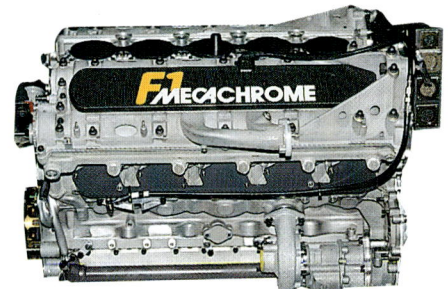

Mecachrome GC37-01
Number of cylinders: 10 in 71deg vee
Capacity: 2999 cc
Power: 760 bhp
Weight: 121 kilos

PLAYLIFE
Benetton

Benetton B198 - Tyres: Bridgestone

The departure last autumn of **the flamboyant Flavio Briatore** certainly marked the end of an era. Moreover, don't you think that the colour scheme of this year's Benetton has lost a little of its previous sparkle? The arrival of **David Richards** at the helm marks the dawn of a new era. And in **Fisichella** and **Wurz** the team has two bright young stars capable of restoring some of the lustre to a team which has never truly recovered from the departure of its prodigal son **Michael Schumacher**. The fact that a number of key technical staff have left has not helped. The Italian-owned team is starting afresh from a solid enough base and aims to return to the top as fast as possible. The presence of **the Mecachrome engine** is a valuable asset during this transition period. The **Benetton B198** was one of the first new cars to be launched and immediately demonstrated great potential. This year, **you'd better count on Benetton** taking the battle to those at the front.

The 1996 Minardi in which he made he made his F1 début never allowed 'Fisico' to make a thunderous start. Halfway through the season he was ousted by a rival who brought along a suitcase full of dollars. Last year Eddie Jordan did not think twice about pairing the young Italian, who had just eight Grands Prix under his belt, with another raw novice - Michael Schumacher's younger brother. Initially the inexperienced Fisichella was shoved aside, in all senses of the word, by 'Schuey Junior' who fears nothing and no one. There was a huge psychological war between the two young guns. Yet from Imola onwards the young Roman made clear his intentions and grasped the initiative. Several podium placings and a number of other good drives allowed Giancarlo to redress the balance. His smile and affability were other factors which enhanced his popularity. In Italy they already consider him to be their next world champion. He has all the right credentials to become one of the superstars of tomorrow. Despite the pressure exerted by Jordan in a bid to hold on to this young talent, Fisichella has transferred this year to Benetton, even though his mentor Flavio Briatore is no longer there. He ought to become a regular fixture on the podium.

Team: **Benetton - Playlife**

Name: **Giancarlo Fisichella**

Number **5**

Date and place of birth: **14 January 1973, Rome (Italy)**
Nationality: Italian
Place of residence: **Monte Carlo**
Marital status: **Single**
Height and weight: **1.72 m / 69 kg**
First GP: Australian GP 1996 (Minardi)
Best position in world championship: **8th in 1997 (Jordan)**
25 GPs, 20 points, 0 wins, 0 pole positions
Italian F3 champion in 1994
Monaco F3 GP winner in 1994
Record in F1: **1996: Minardi, 0 points,**
1997: Jordan , 20 points, 8th in the championship

Personal car? **A Renault Safranne**
Dream car? **The Porsche RS Turbo**
Favourite racing car? **My Formula One cars**
Highlight of racing career? **My second place in the 1997 Belgian Grand Prix**
Worst moment of racing career? **Mugello in 1993, where I had an accident because of brake failure**
Your favourite circuit? **Imola**
Your least favourite circuit? **I don't have one**
Your favourite driver of all time? **Ayrton Senna**
Your favourite current driver? **The stars like Michael Schumacher, Villeneuve, Hakkinen ...**
Favourite food? **Bucatini alla matriciana - pasta from Rome**
Favourite drink? **Coca-Cola and orange juice**
What sports do you take part in? **Football, tennis, jogging, mountain biking and gym work**
Favourite sports? **I like all sports**
Favourite sportsmen? **Alberto Tomba, Paul Gascoigne and Gianluca Vialli**
Favourite type of film? **Comedies**
Favourite actor/actress? **Sylvester Stallone and Sharon Stone**
What do you watch on television? **A little of everything**
What is your favourite colour? **Blue**
Favourite music? **Modern music, particularly Zucchero, Sting and Eros Ramazzotti**
Favourite books? **Motor sport magazines**
Your target in sport? **To become world champion**
Beyond motor sport, who do you admire? **Cindy Crawford...**
If you were left on a desert island, what would you take with you? **Luna, my fiancée**
What is the most important thing in life for you? **My health and to have a happy family**
What do you like most about your profession? **When I'm behind the steering wheel, I'm happy**
What don't you like about your profession? **I don't want any more drives like the end of the 1996 season**
What are your principal strengths? **I am kind**
What are your faults? **I'm not hard enough**
Have you thought about your retirement? **I'd like to stay in motor racing, perhaps even become a team manager**

There are always prophets of gloom who claim that there is no place for lanky drivers in a single-seater. For decades we have been led to believe that tall people have no chance of success.

Alexander got off to a flying start in his bid to disprove that myth. After his win at Le Mans in 1996, he picked up good results in touring-car racing and, with Mercedes, in GT events. Following a promising test at Estoril, he was then signed up as test driver for Benetton. The health problems of his compatriot Gerhard Berger quickly propelled young Wurz to the fore.

He started his F1 career in Canada and by his third race, the British GP, he was finishing on the podium. The capable young deputy certainly made the most of his golden opportunity. This year, along with his team-mate Fisichella, he must put Benetton back on the right road - the one which leads to victory. A driver who has superstitiously worn mismatched boots - one red, one blue - since he scored his very first single-seater victory, the youthfulness of this tall blond Austrian belies his rich experience.

Like Michael Schumacher, his grooming with Mercedes's powerful sports-prototypes has given him top-class technical experience. Alexander Wurz is tipped as a certain champion of the future.

Team: Benetton - Playlife

Name:

Alexander Wurz

Number 6

Date and place of birth: **15 February 1975, Waidhofen/Thaya (Austria)**
Nationality: Austrian
Place of residence: **Monte Carlo**
Marital status: **Engaged to Karin**
Height and weight: 1.87 m / 74 kg
First GP: Canadian GP 1997 (Benetton)
Best position in world championship: **14th in 1997**
Mountain biking world champion in 1986
Austrian F3 champion in 1993
Le Mans winner in 1996
3 GPs, 4 points, 0 wins, 0 pole positions
*Record in F1:***1997: Benetton, 4 points, 14th in the championship**

Personal car? **Renault Laguna station wagon to carry my bikes**
Dream car? **A car that runs without petrol**
Favourite racing car? **The 1992 Formula Ford 1600**
Highlight of racing career? **My victory at Le Mans in 1996**
Worst moment of racing career? **A race for Vauxhall Lotus in Austria in 1992 where I was hot favourite. Because of engine problems I was unable to prove my worth**
Your favourite circuit? **Spa, Laguna Sec and the old Nürburgring**
Your least favourite circuit? **I don't like circuits like Diepholz, which have been built on old aerodromes**
Your favourite driver of all time? **No one in particular**
Your favourite current driver? **Again, no one**
Favourite food? **Italian food, especially pasta**
Favourite drink? **Apple juice with fizzy water**
What sports do you take part in? **Cross country, mountain biking and road cycling**
Favourite sports? **Ice hockey, football**
Favourite sportswoman? **Carl Lewis**
Favourite type of film? **I like all films that make you think, and I hate silly comedies**
Favourite actor? **Bruce Willis and Clint Eastwood**
What do you watch on television? **Star Trek, sport, the adverts and some films**
What is your favourite colour? **The colours on my helmet, mainly blue**
Favourite music? **I love everything from classical to heavy rock**
Favourite books? **Political and news magazines and some novels**
Your target in sport? **To drive flat out to the maximum of my ability**
Beyond motor sport, who do you admire? **As yet, I have not had the time to think about it!**
If you were left on a desert island, what would you take with you? **My fiancée Karin, a knife and some water**
What is the most important thing in life for you? **Health and happiness**
What do you like most about your profession? **Driving to the limit**
What don't you like about your profession? **Not having enough free time**
What are your principal strengths? **I am relaxed**
What are your faults? **That's difficult to say**
Have you thought about your retirement? **I'd take a whole year to go round the world stopping when I felt like it and enjoying the freedom**

PLUS POINTS:

- Top-line drivers
- Adrian Newey's design skills
- The Mercedes engine
- Bridgestone tyre gamble
- Excellent budget

MINUS POINTS:

- Neither driver has number one status
- Engine reliability could be better
- Outrageous ambition
- Late launch of the MP4-13

Managing director:
Ron Dennis

Technical director:
Adrian Newey

Address: McLaren International Ltd
Woking Business Park, Albert Drive
Woking, Surrey GU21 5JY, Great Britain
Tel: 00 44 1483 72 82 11
Fax: 00 44 1483 72 01 57
Internet: www.mclaren.co.uk
Size of workforce: 220
First GP: Monaco 1966
Number of Grands Prix: 460
Number of wins: 107
Number of pole positions: 80
Number of points scored: 2049.5
World constructors' titles: 7 (1974,84,85,88,89,90 91)
World drivers' titles: (Fittipaldi 1974, Hunt 1976, Lauda 1984, Prost 1985-86-89, Senna 1988-90-91)
Test driver: Ricardo Zonta (Brazil)

1997 result: 4th (63 points)

McLaren
MERCEDES

McLaren MP4-13 - Tyres: Bridgestone

Mercedes-Benz FO 110G V10
Number of cylinders: 10 in 72deg vee
Capacity: 2998 cc
Power: 770 bhp
Weight: 107 kilos

In 1988 **the McLaren Hondas of Senna and Prost** absolutely dominated the championship, winning all but one of the 16 races. Since Honda pulled out of F1 at the end of 1992, it has taken **Ron Dennis's team** a little while to get back on the right track. Today, a partnership with **Mercedes** has once again elevated **McLaren** to a position of towering strength. **A brilliant V10**, an engineer of renown snaffled from **Williams**, two quick and experienced drivers and a thoroughly well-drilled team have combined to put **McLaren** back at the head of the pack. The **MP4-13** was developed after no less than 12,000 hours in the wind tunnel. Their interpretation of the rules has also allowed them to have fine-tuned a driver-operated individual wheel-braking system which confers better traction when cornering. In Melbourne **the Silver Arrows** monopolised the front row of the grid and went on to run rings around their opposition. Hotly tipped before the championship had kicked off, the Mercedes-powered McLarens of **Hakkinen** and **Coulthard** are already a major thorn in the sides of Williams, Ferrari and Benetton.

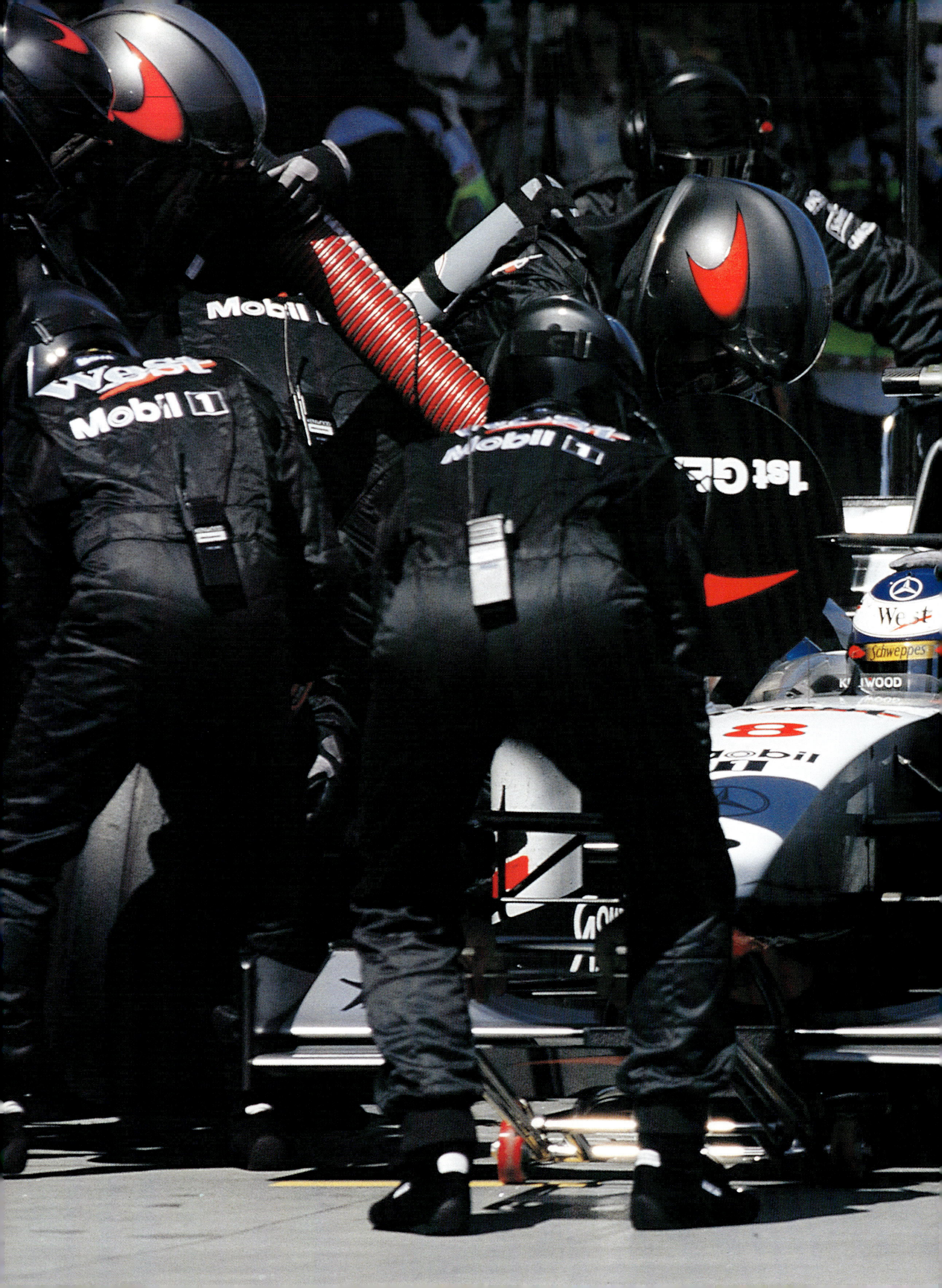
Mobil
West
Mobil 1
Mobil 1
West
Schweppes

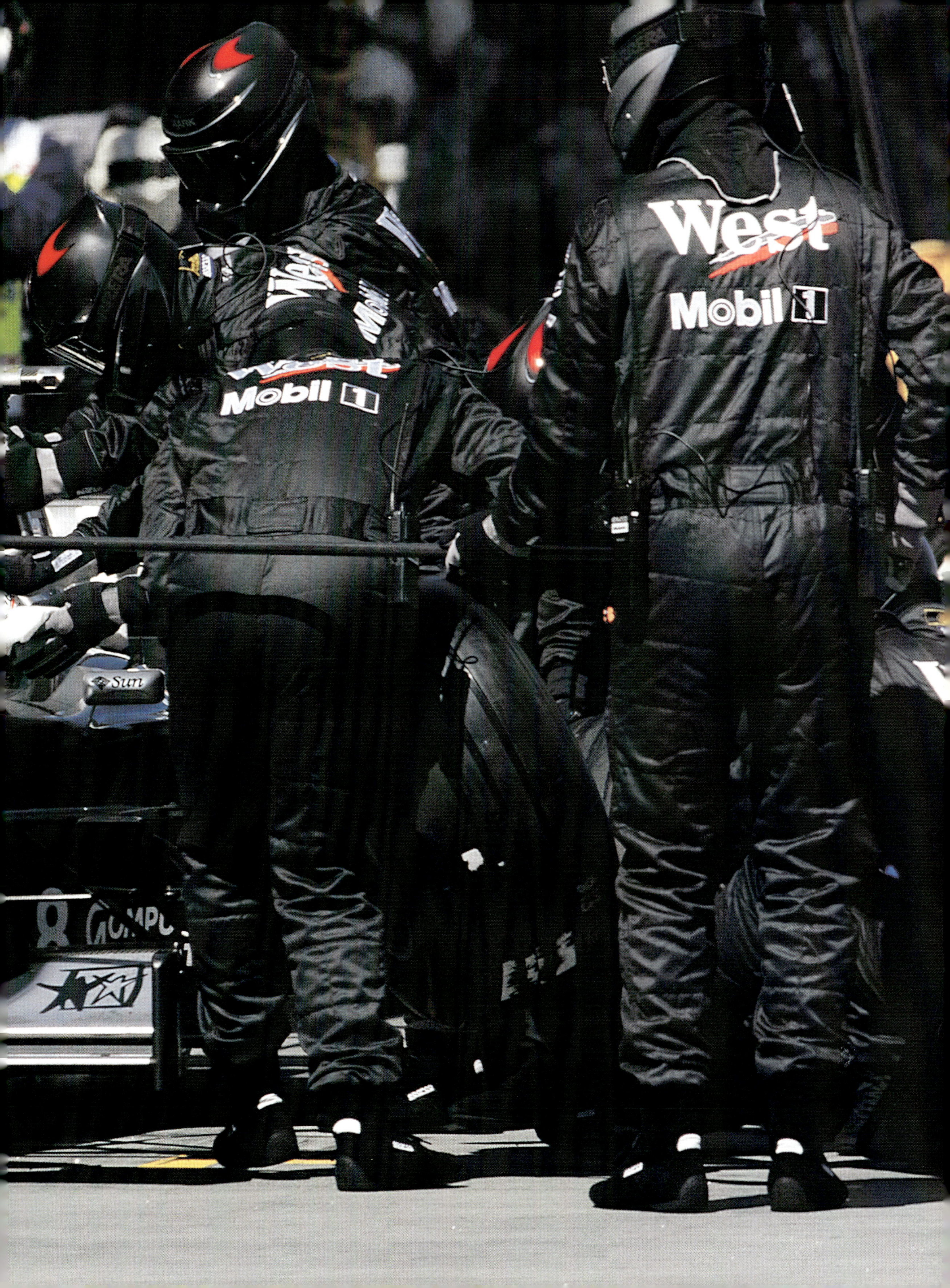
West
Mobil 1
West
Mobil 1
Sun

This handsome Scot comes from a good family and can often be distinguished by his kilt at big nights out. He came to Formula One in 1994, taking the place of the late Ayrton Senna at Williams. Despite finishing third in the championship in 1995, the arrival of Villeneuve steered him towards McLaren the following season and he enjoyed a productive collaboration with Alain Prost, then the team's adviser. Thanks to the potency of the Mercedes engines, the famous English team quickly pulled itself round after a spell of poor results and David Coulthard did not miss the opportunity to make his intentions clear. Following Michael Schumacher's disqualification, he was classified third in the 1997 world championship, having won both the Australian and Italian Grands Prix. At 27 years of age, his best is still perhaps to come. He is the master of the perfect start. By contrast, his over-exuberance has sometimes played nasty tricks on him. As with Hakkinen, the return to the fore of the McLaren team gives him a formidable springboard towards success. Always good humoured and philosophical about failure, his taste for jokes has endeared him to many. This Scotsman could well follow in the footsteps of his compatriot Jackie Stewart, with whose team he learned the ropes in Formula Opel, F3 and F3000 from 1990-1992.

Team : **McLaren - Mercedes**

Name : **David Coulthard**

Number 7

Date and place of birth: **27 March 1971, Twynholm (Scotland)**
Nationality: British
Place of residence: **Monte Carlo**
Marital status: **Single**
Height and weight: **1.82 m / 75 kg**
First GP: Spanish GP 1994 (Williams)
Best position in world championship: **3rd in 1995 (Williams) and 1997 (McLaren)**
58 GPs, 117 points, 3 wins, 5 pole positions.
Formula Ford junior champion in 1989
Record in F1: **1994: Williams, 14 points, 8th in the championship, 1995: Williams, 49 points, 3rd, 1996: McLaren, 18 points, 7th, 1997: McLaren, 36 points, 3rd**

Personal car? **An M-class Mercedes and an SLK**
Dream car? **The McLaren F1 road car**
Favourite racing car? **The 1994 Williams and the McLarens I have driven**
Highlight of racing career? **Difficult to say, probably my victory in Melbourne in 1997**
Worst moment of racing career? **My accident in the Opel Lotus at Spa in 1990**
Your favourite circuit? **Spa, it's fantastic**
Your least favourite circuit? **Budapest**
Your favourite driver of all time? **Clark, Prost, Mansell and Senna**
Your favourite current driver? **Nobody in particular**
Favourite food? **Authentic Italian pasta**
Favourite drink? **Tea and mineral water**
What sports do you take part in? **Golf, running, cycling and swimming**
Favourite sports? **Athletics**
Favourite sportsman? **Linford Christie**
Favourite type of film? **I love going to the cinema and I like action films best**
Favourite actors? **Stallone, Schwarzenegger, Mel Gibson and Sean Connery**
What do you watch on television? **I don't watch it**
What is your favourite colour? **Blue**
Favourite music? **I like Texas, Bon Jovi, Aerosmith, Guns and Roses, Queen, Phil Collins and the Irish group Coors - but I can't stand rap!**
Favourite books? **Nothing in particular**
Your target in sport? **It was always my dream to be a Formula One driver**
Beyond motor sport, who do you admire? **Linford Christie for his famous 100-metre races and Sean Connery in James Bond films**
If you were left on a desert island, what would you take with you? **My family**
What is the most important thing in life for you? **My health**
What do you like most about your profession? **The speed**
What don't you like about your profession? **It's too political**
What are your principal strengths? **You'd have to ask other people**
What are your faults? **There are too many of them. You'd have to make a list**
Have you thought about your retirement? **I'll go back to Scotland!**

'The Finn', as he always likes to append each of his fan's autographs, has already taken part in almost 100 Grands Prix.

When he won the last race of the 1997 season at Jerez, he finally broke a run of bad luck which had bedevilled him, often when he was in the lead. Fortunately there is justice in this sport.

When he first joined McLaren in 1993, he had to make do with a test-driving role, as Michael Andretti was partnering Senna in the race team.

When the American quit F1 and returned to the States, Mika was promoted and promptly outqualified his illustrious team-mate first time out! The Flying Finn has a flamboyant style.

In Australia in 1993, he flew through the air for several metres after taking off over a kerb, fortunately without serious consequences.

In November 1995, again in Australia, he suffered a terrible head injury, but was back behind the wheel four months later after showing an incredible blend of courage and will-power. Now restored to full fitness, and perhaps even stronger than before, he has become one of the true superstars of Formula One.

Team: McLaren - Mercedes

Number 8

Name: Mika Hakkinen

Date and place of birth: **28 September 1968, Helsinki (Finland)**
Nationality: **Finnish**
Place of residence: **Monte Carlo**
Marital status: **Single**
Height and weight: **1.79 m / 69 kg**
First GP: **USA GP 1991 (Lotus)**
Best position in world championship: **4th in 1994 (McLaren)**
96 GPs, 118 points, 1 win, 1 pole position
Formula Ford champion in 1987
British F3 champion in 1990
Record in F1: 1991: **Lotus, 2 points, 15th in the championship, 1992: Lotus, 11 points, 8th , 1993: McLaren, 4 points, 15th, 1994: McLaren, 26 points, 4th, 1995: McLaren, 17 points, 7th 1996: McLaren, 31 points, 5th , 1997: McLaren, 27 points, 5th**

Personal car? **A V-class Mercedes to transport my kart and an SLK**
Dream car? **Ferraris and Mercedes**
Favourite racing car? **All the McLaren F1 cars that I have driven**
Highlight of racing career? **My pole position at the Nürburgring on my birthday and, of course, my first F1 win at Jerez, both in 1997**
Worst moment of racing career? **Imola in 1994 and my accident in Adelaide in 1995**
Your favourite circuit? **Monaco, it's a legendary circuit**
Your least favourite circuit? **Montreal**
Your favourite driver of all time? **No one in particular**
Your favourite current driver? **I haven't got one of those either**
Favourite food? **Meat balls**
Favourite drink? **Water, tea and Coca-Cola**
What sports do you take part in? **Jogging, swimming, skiing, tennis and jet-skiing**
Favourite sports? **Alpine skiing, tennis and golf**
Favourite sportsmen? **The footballer Jari Litmanen, the ski jumper Andreas Goldberger and myself ...** (smiles)
Favourite type of film? **Horror films, and recently I enjoyed the latest James Bond**
Favourite actors? **Bruce Willis, Schwarzenegger and Stallone.**
What do you watch on television? **Sports programmes**
What is your favourite colour? **Dark blue and black**
Favourite music? **Dire Staits, Phil Collins and Michael Jackson**
Favourite books? **Novels.**
Your target in sport? **To be world champion**
Beyond motor sport, who do you admire? **Skiers and jockeys**
If you were left on a desert island, what would you take with you? **A telephone**
What is the most important thing in life for you? **My health**
What do you like most about your profession? **The competition**
What don't you like about your profession? **Accidents**
What are your principal strengths? **A good sense of humour**
What are your faults? **Too many to mention!**
Have you thought about your retirement? **No**

PLUS POINTS:

- On the verge of better things
- The deal with Mugen-Honda
- The arrival of Damon Hill
- No-nonsense style of Ralf Schumacher

MINUS POINTS:

- Doubts over reliability of the Mugen-Honda
- The rapport between the two drivers?
- The loss of the Peugeot engine

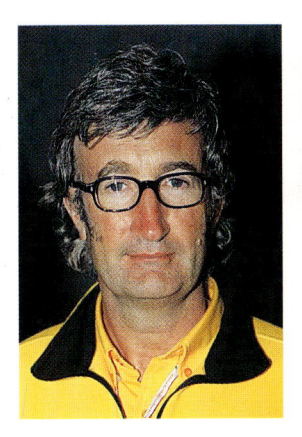

Managing director:
Eddie Jordan

Technical director:
Gary Anderson

Address: Jordan Grand Prix Ltd
Buckingham Road, Silverstone,
Northamptonshire NN12 8TJ, Great Britain
Tel: 00 44 1327 85 71 53
Fax: 00 44 1327 85 21 20
Internet: www.jordangp.com
Size of workforce: 148
First GP: United States 1991 (Phoenix)
Number of Grands Prix: 114
Number of pole positions: 1
Number of points scored: 121
Best result in world constructors' championship: 5th (1991, 1994, 1996 and 1997)
Best result in world drivers' championship: Barrichello, 6th in 1994
Test driver: Pedro de la Rosa (Spain)

1997 result: 5th (33 points)

MUGEN-HONDA
Jordan

Jordan 198 - Tyres: Goodyear

Mugen-Honda MF 301HC
Number of cylinders:
10 in 72deg vee
Capacity: 3000 cc
Power: 730 bhp
Weight: 135 kilos

While some teams have placed great faith in the importance of continuity, **Eddie Jordan's outfit** has done completely the opposite. **After losing Peugeot**, Jordan picked up a **new engine deal with Mugen Honda** - and he also signed up 1996 world champion **Damon Hill**. Having sometimes struggled to restrain the youthful enthusiasm of **Fisichella** and **Ralf Schumacher** the previous year, the wily Irishman has changed his strategy. The presence of the enormously experienced Hill will be a massive asset for a team which is still waiting to release its full potential. For the moment **the relationship between Hill and the younger Schumacher** is working well. The **Jordan 198** might have been slightly off the pace at the start of the year, but the hornet (which has replaced the snake on the re-liveried yellow car's nose) will surely deliver its sting in due course.

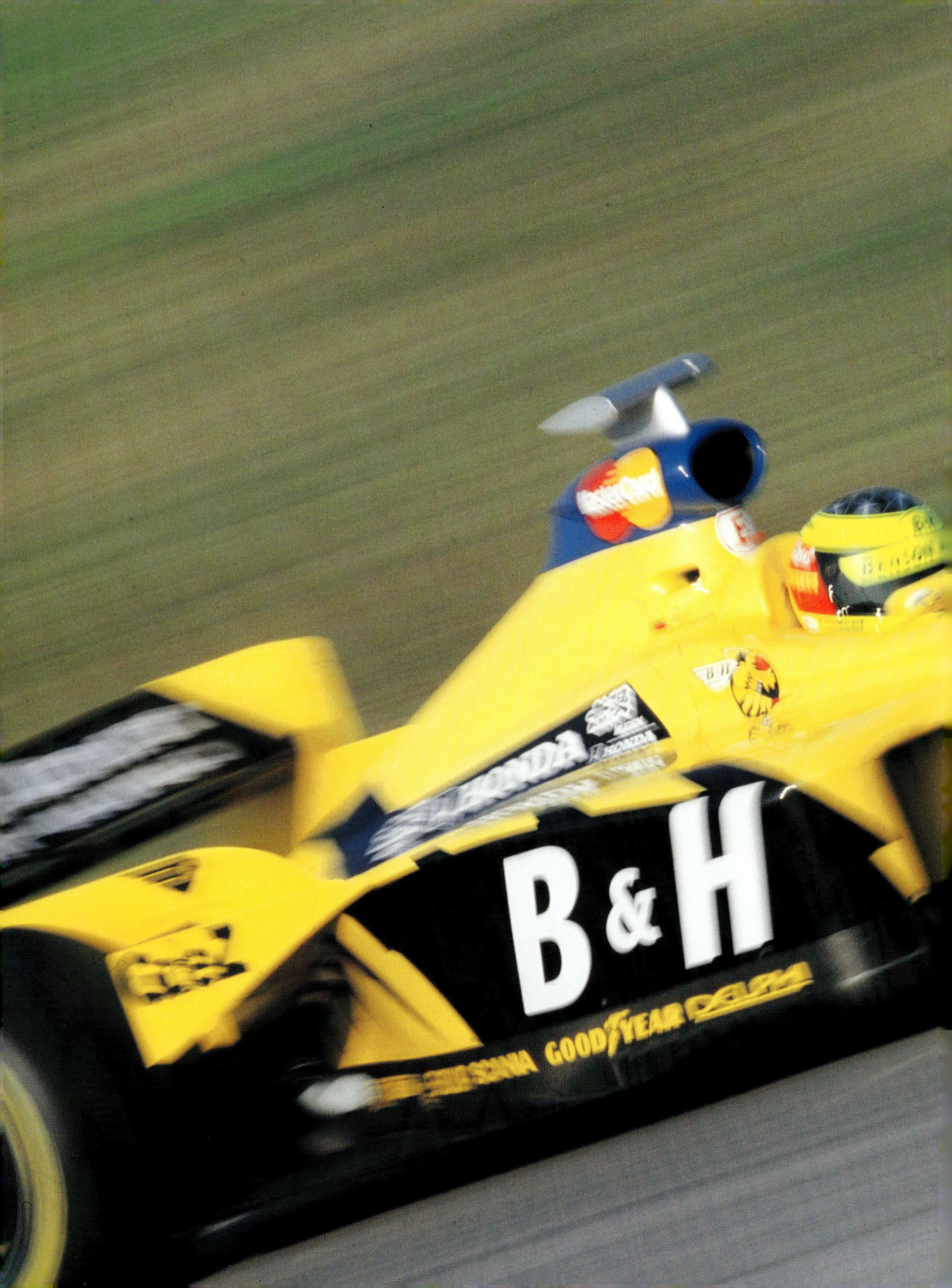
B & H
GOODYEAR
SCANIA
HONDA

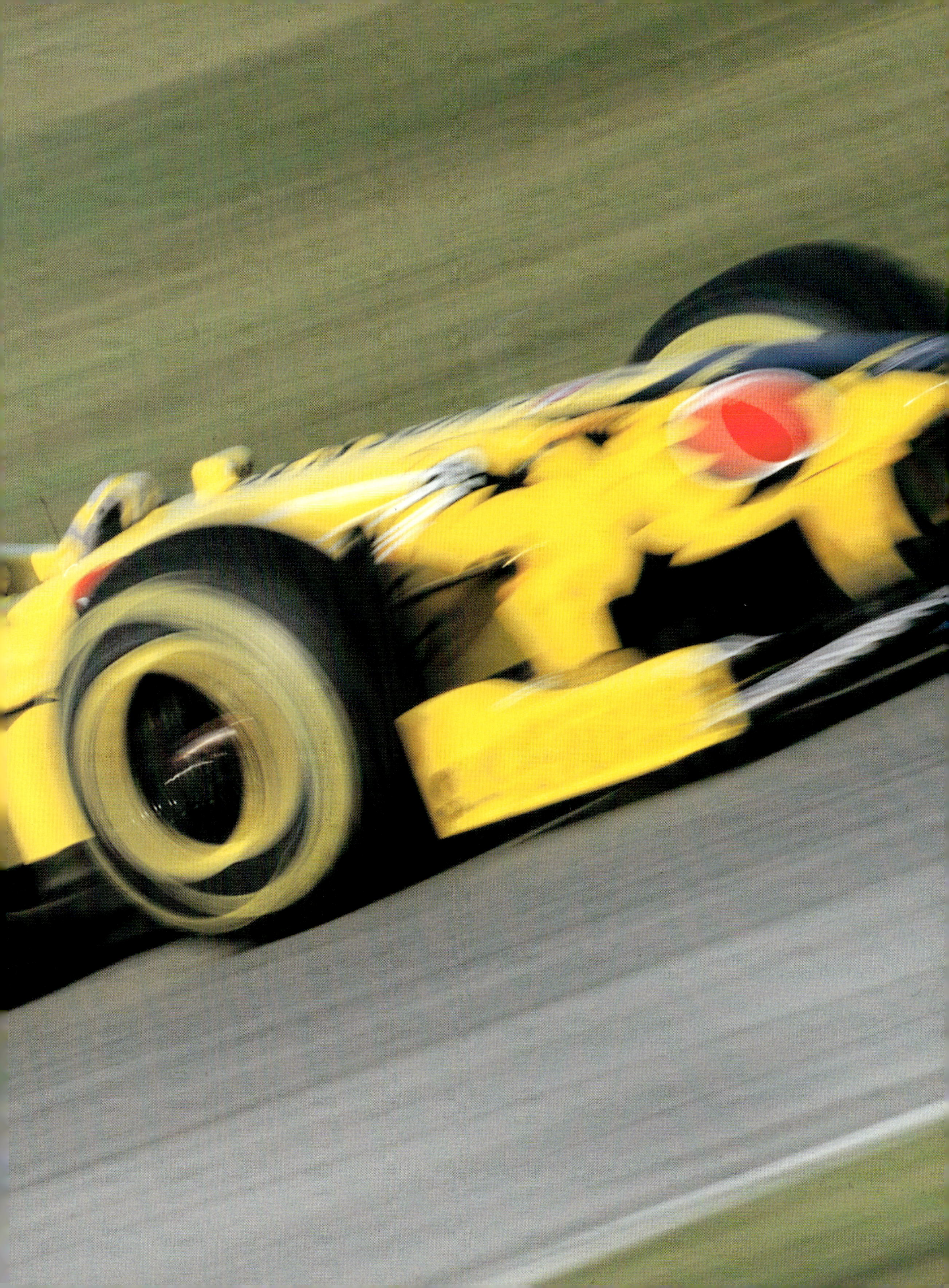

Wooed last summer by everyone, Damon Hill dismissed the overtures of Sauber, McLaren and Prost and succumbed to those of the Jordan team. Having gambled entirely on youth in 1997, wily old campaigner Eddie Jordan has changed tack for the new season. The enormous experience of the 1996 world champion was a persuasive argument for having him in the team. After the splendour of his career at Williams, it had taken a great deal of courage and self-belief for him to sign for Arrows, where he often found himself in the lower reaches of the grid, among the also-rans, with little prospect of making the finish. Although transformed by Tom Walkinshaw, Arrows was never able to provide Damon with the right ammunition to perform at his true level. His exploits in Budapest could not have been better. In the closing moments of the race, Villeneuve deprived his former team-mate of what would have been an extraordinary triumph. The popularity of the British driver peaked after this remarkable performance.

In what was almost a sabbatical year, this discreet individual showed his true worth. His self-sacrifice, his professionalism and his desire to plunder two or three thousandths of a second to climb to the eighth row of the starting grid showed that the former champion's motivation is still there. Many former world champions have left the racing scene happy with the money they have made. Jordan marks the start of a new adventure for Damon. Hopefully his relationship with the younger Schumacher will not be too tempestuous. After the unveiling of the Jordan Mugen-Honda 198 at the Royal Albert Hall in London, a smiling Damon said: 'I am led to believe that, more than anything, Ralf wants to beat his brother - so we shall do it together!' With the brio of the young German and the experience of his British driver, Eddie Jordan's astute management has taken the team to the threshold of success. Knowing Damon, he will still find the time for a little rock 'n' roll and a few rounds of golf!

Team: Jordan - Mugen - Honda

Name:
Damon Hill

Number 9

Date and place of birth: **17 September 1960, London**
Nationality: British
Place of residence: Dublin
Marital status: **Married to Georgie, four children (Oliver, Joshua, Tabatha and Rosy)**
Height and weight: **1.82 m / 70 kg**
First GP: British GP 1992 (Brabham)
84 GPs, 21 wins, 333 points, 20 pole positions
World champion in 1996 (Williams)
Second twice in 1994 and 1995 (Williams)
Record in F1: **1992: Brabham 0 points,**
1993: Williams 69 points, 3rd in the championship,
1994: Williams 91 points, 2nd, 1995: Williams 69 points, 2nd ,
1996: Williams 97 points, world champion, 1997: Arrows 7 points, 12th

Personal car? **Honda Shuttle**
Dream car? **Porsche Turbo**
Favourite racing car? **The Williams FW15 with active suspension**
Highlight of racing career? **My victories at Silverstone in 1994 and Suzuka in 1996**
Worst moment of racing career? **Imola 1994**
Your favourite circuit? **Brands Hatch and Macau**
Your least favourite circuit? **I don't like Montreal very much**
Your favourite driver of all time? **Lauda, Prost, Mansell and Senna**
Your favourite current driver? **Alesi and Hakkinen**
Favourite food? **English cooking and roast chicken**
Favourite drink? **Beer and wine, but not mixed!**
What sports do you take part in? **Jogging, going to the gym and golf**
Favourite sports? **Surfing, athletics, skiing and golf**
Who is your favourite sportsman? **Downhill skiers like Klammer or Killy**
Favourite type of film? **Woody Allen films**
Favourite actors? **I love any film with Jack Nicholson, Robert de Niro or Lauren Bacall**
What do you watch on television? **Sport and contemporary English comedy**
What is your favourite colour? **Red**
Favourite music? **Actually, I like The Verve, Cake, Iggy Pop, Van Morrison and The Beatles**
Favourite books? **Autobiographies and books by Martin Amis**
Your target in sport? **To enjoy myself**
Beyond motor sport, who do you admire? **People who look after handicapped children**
If you were left on a desert island, what would you take with you? **A guitar and a surf board**
What is the most important thing in life for you? **To be with my family and friends**
What do you like most about your profession? **The spirit of competition**
What don't you like about your profession? **The danger**
What are your principal strengths? **That's not for me to say**
What are your faults? **I don't think that I achieve all I could**
Have you thought about your retirement? **I'd like to go back to school and learn all the things I missed out on first time round, especially English!**

Assisted by his surname, Ralf Schumacher has not taken long to join his brother in Formula One.
His arrival at Jordan was dramatic. In the space of a few races he completely overwhelmed his team-mate Fisichella, who swiftly lost his way. Schumacher was dominant in every respect. He gained his first podium finish in the Argentinian Grand Prix, after having pushed his young Italian colleague off the track. It was a considerable strain for Eddie Jordan to keep the peace between his two charges.

The young Schumacher did not respond well to the pressure and his propensity for errors increased. During this time, 'Fisico' calmly asserted his superiority. This young German is still short of experience. Although spirited and very quick, he lacks consistency. In the Luxembourg Grand Prix, he clashed with his brother and denied him precious points. The reassuring presence of his new team-mate Damon Hill should enable him to acquire the maturity he still lacks, and which has been his only fault. And that'll be the day when former world champion Hill will have to worry. When he started 25 years ago, Jody Scheckter was like a bull in a china shop, causing havoc everywhere. When he learned to stay on the track, he started to win races and ultimately the title. Ralf could quite easily follow the same path - he has both the talent and the self-belief. There could soon be one Schumacher hiding behind another!

Team: Jordan - Mugen - Honda
Name: Ralf Schumacher
Number 10

Date and place of birth: **30 June 1975, Hürth (Germany)**
Nationality: German
Place of residence: Monte Carlo
Marital status: **Single**
Height and weight: **1.78 m / 73 kg**
First GP: **Australian GP 1997 (Jordan)**
Best position in world championship: **11th in 1997 (Jordan)**
Macau F3 winner in 1995
Japanese Formula Nippon champion in 1996
Record in F1: **1997: Jordan, 13 points, 11th in the championship**

Personal car? **Honda Prelude**
Dream car? **Porsche Carrera RS Turbo**
Favourite racing car? **This year's Jordan, of course**
Highlight of racing career? **The 1995 Macau F3 race, the 1996 Formula Nippon championship and, of course, my first podium finish in Argentina in 1997**
Worst moment of racing career? **Spa and Monaco in 1997**
Your favourite circuit? **I like to drive, therefore I like all the circuits, especially Monaco**
Your least favourite circuit? **None**
Your favourite driver of all time? **Nobody in particular**
Your favourite current driver? **My brother Michael and Coulthard**
Favourite food? **Pasta**
Favourite drink? **Apple juice with fizzy water**
What sports do you take part in? **Tennis, karting and fitness**
Favourite sports? **Basketball, athletics and the Olympic Games**
Favourite sportsmen? **High-risk sportsmen**
Favourite type of film? **Action movies and *Titanic* which I thought was terrific**
Favourite actors? **Bill Cosby**
What do you watch on television? **I like television a lot but I don't watch anything in particular**
What is your favourite colour? **Dark colours**
Favourite music? **Light rock and the music from *Titanic***
Favourite books? **I don't like reading, except Tom Clancy novels**
Your target in sport? **First of all to make the podium, then to win and then …**
Beyond motor sport, who do you admire? **My brother and my family**
If you were left on a desert island, what would you take with you? **A boat so that I could leave quickly**
What is the most important thing in life for you? **My health, to be happy, to win lots of money and to succeed in whatever I do**
What do you like most about your profession? **Driving**
What don't you like about your profession? **I like it all. I am 21 years old, I'm open-minded. We shall see later on**
What are your principal strengths? **That's not for me to say. But I'm very strong mentally**
What are your faults? **I'm too egotistical**
Have you thought about your retirement? **I'll go karting at Kerpen with my brother Michael**

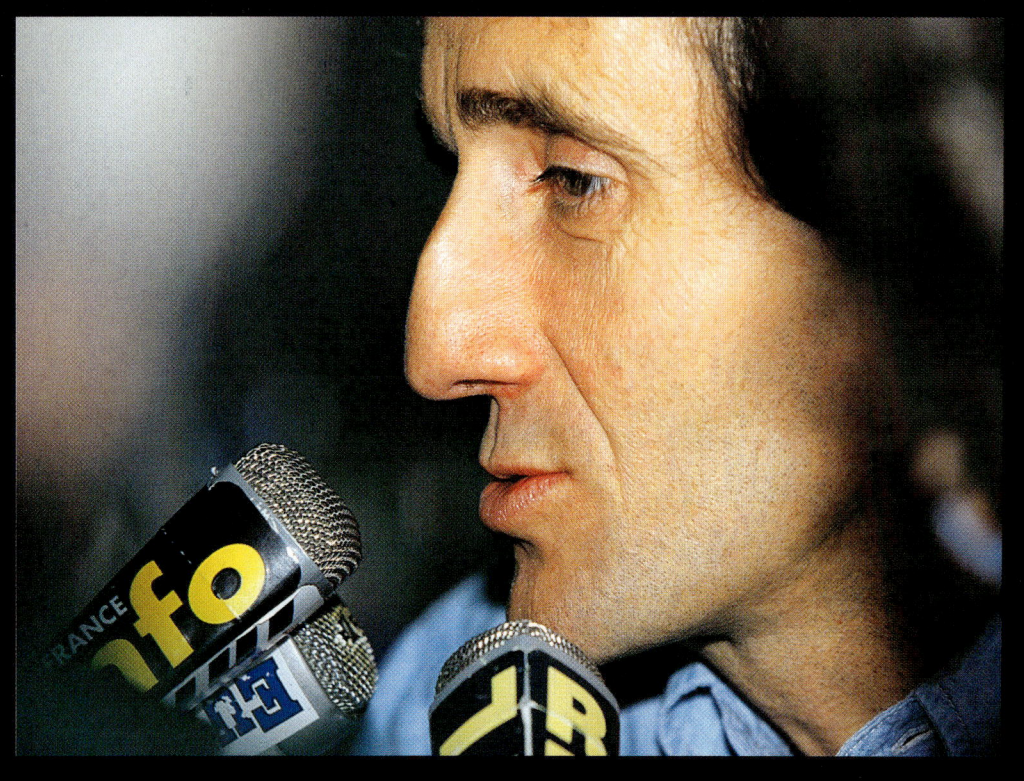

PLUS POINTS:

- Good budget
- A team in the process of rapid evolution
- Strong technical staff
- The presence of Alain Prost
- Top-class drivers
- The Peugeot engine

MINUS POINTS:

- Relocation of the factory during the course of the season
- Still a little short of experience

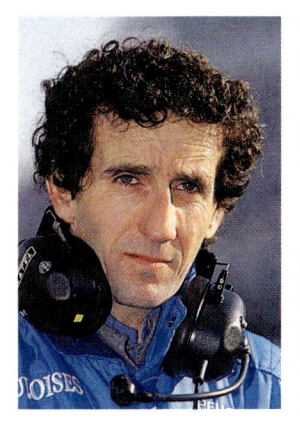

Managing director:
Alain Prost

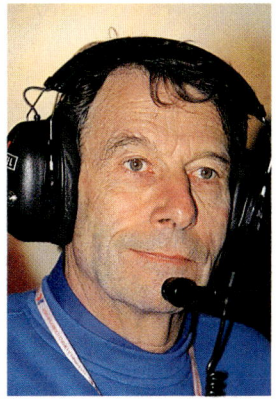

Technical director:
Bernard Dudot

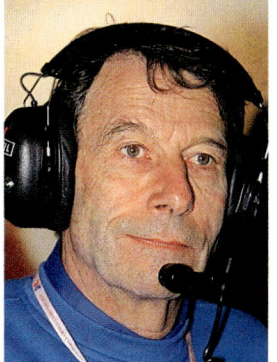

Address: Prost Grand Prix, Quartier des Sangliers, 7, Av. Eugène Freyssinet, 78280, France
Tel: 00 33 1 39 30 11 00
Fax: 00 33 1 39 30 11 01
Internet: www.peugeot.com/v10
Size of workforce: 150
First GP: Ligier (Brazil 1976), Prost (Australia 1997)
Number of Grands Prix: Ligier (326), Prost (17)
Number of wins: 9 (Ligier)
Number of pole positions: 9 (Ligier)
Number of points scored: 389 (Ligier), 21 (Prost)
Best result in world constructors' championship:
2nd in 1980 (Ligier), 6th in 1997 (Prost)
Best result in world drivers' championship: Laffite 4th in 1979-80-81 for Ligier and Panis 9th in 1997 for Prost.

1997 result: 6th (21 points)

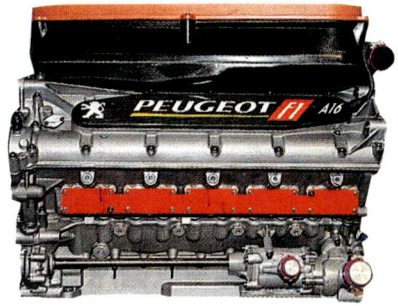

Peugeot A16
Number of cylinders: 10 in 72deg vee
Capacity: 2998 cc
Power: 750 bhp
Weight: 125 kilos

Prost AP01 - Tyres: Bridgestone

PEUGEOT
Prost

Handicapped by an endless series of transmission problems during its gestation, the **Prost AP-01** was not exactly on peak form in Australia.
Alain Prost had made it clear before the start of the campaign that the first three races would be tough. Still not fully fine-tuned, despite the best efforts of **Panis** and **Trulli**, the front of the grid is still out of reach for 'les bleus', as the French fondly call them.
But with strong financial resources and **a terrific new partnership with Peugeot**, the evolving **Prost GP team** can look to the future with optimism.
Once the South American races are over, **Alain Prost** will himself get back behind the wheel to see what effect the new regulations have had. He is honest enough to admit that he is a little out of touch. After that, the Prosts should work their way into points-scoring positions while awaiting even better things.

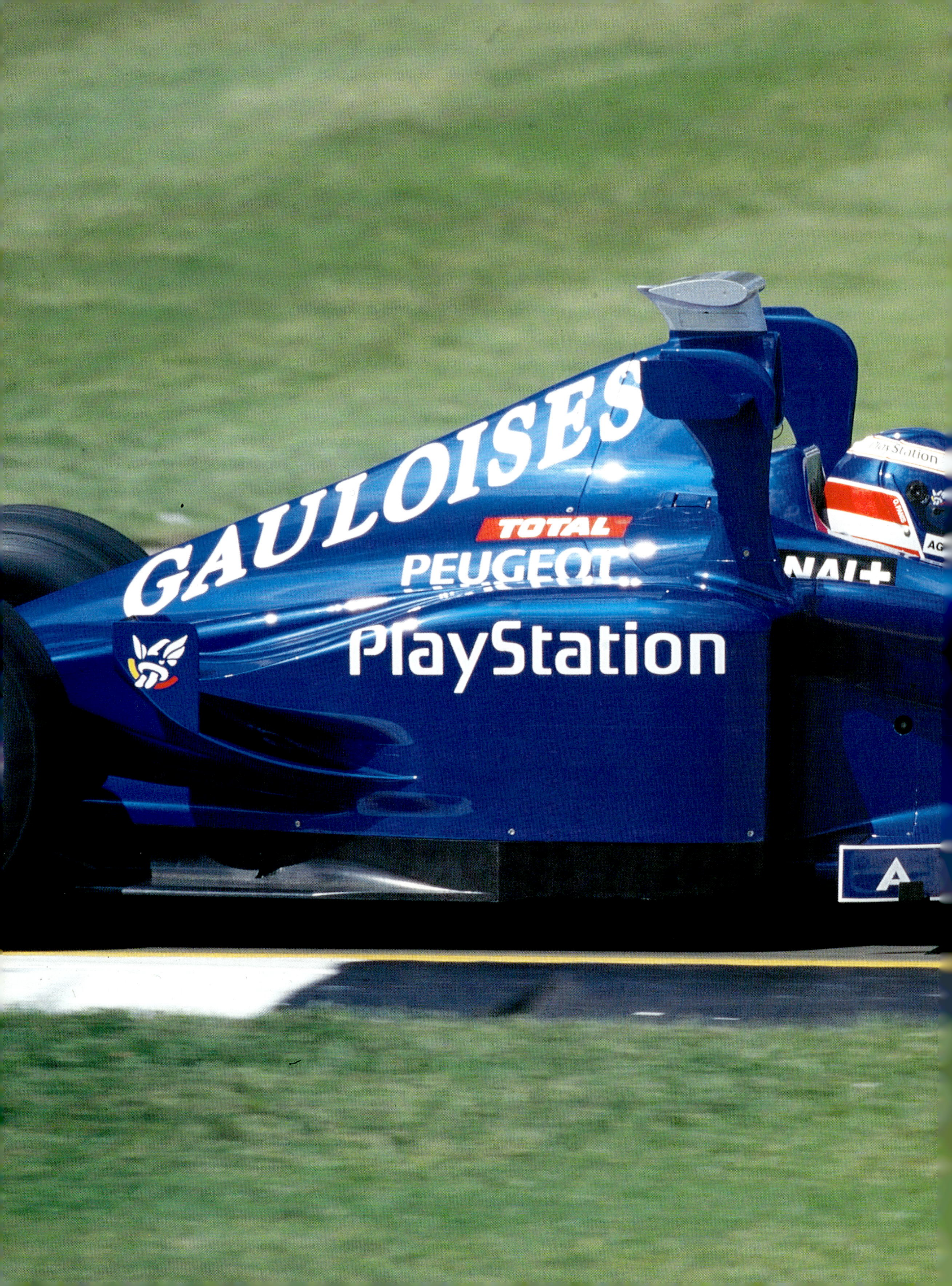
GAULOISES
TOTAL
PEUGEOT
PlayStation

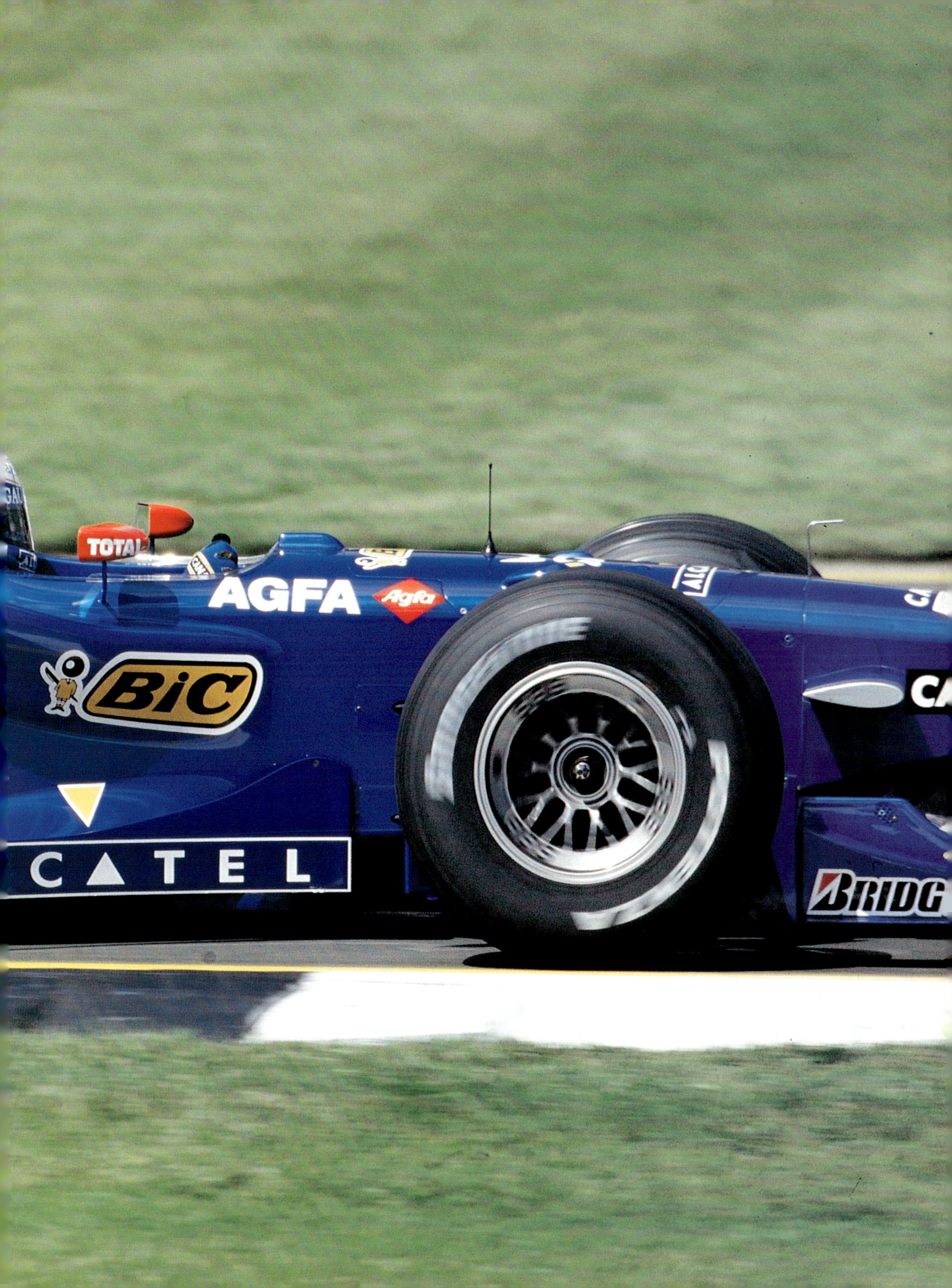
TOTAL
AGFA
Agfa
BiC
CATEL

Olivier Panis approaches his fifth season in Formula One with a new-found confidence. The victim of a serious crash in Montreal last year, he has shown remarkable courage while recovering full use of his shattered legs. Just 103 days after the accident he was back on the track and finishing sixth in the Luxembourg Grand Prix. Throughout his convalescence an avalanche of get-well messages served notice of his great popularity. Today, completely rehabilitated, and as sharp physically as he is mentally, he is ready to take on the fantastic challenge of the Prost Grand Prix team. He has a perfect relationship with those around him - and with Alain Prost in particular. For Olivier, the word 'team' really means something. He constantly stresses the importance of his relationship with his partner Trulli if they are going to have a successful time with the Prost AP-01. The French driver is both mature and optimistic. After a brilliant start to 1997, he was lying third in the world championship before his terrible accident at the Canadian Grand Prix. This year, feeling even stronger and with a competitive car at his disposal, Olivier has everything he needs to succeed. He knows the taste of victory and is impatient to savour it again. Quite apart from his skill at the wheel, his awareness of the importance of human relationships, his polite manners and his ready availability in a world of constant demands ought to make him one of Formula One's leading lights.

Team: Prost - Peugeot

Name: **Olivier Panis**

Number **11**

Date and place of birth: **2 September 1966, Lyon (France)**
Nationality: **French**
Place of residence: **Varces, near Grenoble (France)**
Marital status: **Married to Anne, one child, Aurélien**
Height and weight: **1.73 m / 76 kg**
First GP: **Brazilian GP 1994 (Ligier)**
Best position in world championship: **8th in 1995 (Ligier)**
French Formula Renault champion in 1989
FIA F3000 champion in 1993
59 GPs, 70 points, 1 win, 0 pole positions
Record in F1: 1994: Ligier, 9 points, 11th in the championship, 1995: Ligier, 16 points, 8th, 1996: Ligier, 13 points, 9th, 1997: Prost, 16 points, 9th

Personal car? **Peugeot 406 Coupé**
Dream car? **Lamborghini Diablo**
Favourite racing car? **All the Formula One cars that I have driven, and the 1997 Prost**
Highlight of racing career? **My victory at Monaco in 1996, obviously**
Worst moment of racing career? **Imola in 1994 and my accident at Montreal in 1997**
Your favourite circuit? **Paul Ricard**
Your least favourite circuit? **None**
Your favourite driver of all time? **Prost and Senna**
Your favourite current driver? **I've a lot of respect for the driving of Schumacher**
Favourite food? **Pasta**
Favourite drink? **Water and Coca-Cola**
What sports do you take part in? **Jogging, cycling, gym work and karting**
Favourite sports? **Football**
Favourite sportsmen? **None in particular**
Favourite type of film? **Comedies like *The Visitors* and adventure films**
Favourite actor/actress? **Dustin Hoffmann and Julia Roberts**
What do you watch on television? **Films and *Les Guignols de L'Info* (French equivalent of *Spitting Image*)**
What is your favourite colour? **Blue**
Favourite music? **Compilation CDs, and the current hits**
Favourite books? **Sports magazines**
Your target in sport? **To be the Formula One world champion**
Beyond motor sport, who do you admire? **My father**
If you were left on a desert island, what would you take with you? **My family**
What is the most important thing in life for you? **Honesty**
What do you like most about your profession? **I am currently carrying out my childhood dream. I love to master a machine, to be at the limit**
What don't you like about your profession? **Political problems within the sport carry far too much importance**
What are your principal strengths? **That's for my wife and friends to say**
What are your faults? **The same answer as above**
Have you thought about your retirement? **No, not yet**

The rise of Jarno Trulli has been meteoric. He was quickly snapped up by former Benetton boss Flavio Briatore and he did not have to wait long for his break. In less than 18 months, he passed from karting to Formula One with only one season in F3 to familiarise himself with single-seater racing. At Minardi he learned the ropes quietly and happily until the day of Olivier Panis's accident. Alain Prost needed a driver to fill the gap and picked Trulli in preference to Emmanuel Collard. Regarded as the team's number one driver, he learned very quickly. In Austria, in his last race before Panis's return, he was third on the grid and led the race convincingly for 37 laps before engine failure put him out. While looking for a job in 1998, he was desperately keen to carry on his relationship with Prost GP. It was a fantastic experience for him to work with the four-time world champion and in the autumn his dream became a reality. With Olivier Panis he is ready to take the team to the very top. The young Italian from Pescara declared: 'This year I am going to win races and also try to learn French! I am very keen to learn from such masters as Alain Prost, Bernard Dudot and Olivier Panis.' A veritable ball of energy, seldom able to keep still, he discovers true tranquillity the moment he lowers the visor of his crash helmet. With Fisichella and Trulli the Italian tifosi are going to have something to shout about. The potential is certainly there.

Team: Prost - Peugeot

Name:
Jarno Trulli

Number 12

Date and place of birth: **13 July 1974, Pescara (Italy)**
Nationality: Italian
Place of residence: Francavilla (Italy)
Marital status: **Single**
Height and weight: **1.73 m / 60 kg**
First GP: Australian GP 1997 (Minardi)
Best position in world championship: **15th in 1997 (Prost)**
14 GPs, 3 points, 0 wins, 0 pole positions
German F3 champion in 1996
Record in F1: **1997: Minardi and Prost: 3 points, 15th in the championship**

Personal car? **Peugeot 406 Coupé**
Dream car? **I don't have one**
Favourite racing car? **My F3 Dallara in 1996 and the Prost**
Highlight of racing career? **My first points at Hockenheim in 1997 and also Zeltweg where I led the race for more than 30 laps**
Worst moment of racing career? **Budapest in 1997 where nothing went right**
Your favourite circuit? **Hockenheim. I have always been lucky there both in F3 and F1**
Your least favourite circuit? **Monte Carlo. I don't like driving there, it is too small for F1**
Your favourite driver of all time? **Niki Lauda**
Your favourite current driver? **Damon Hill**
Favourite food? **Pizza**
Favourite drink? **Coca-Cola**
What sports do you take part in? **Cycling, jogging and gym work**
Favourite sports? **Alpine skiing, motor racing and karting**
Favourite sportsmen? **Alberto Tomba and Max Biaggi**
Favourite type of film? **I don't often go to the cinema but I like detective thrillers and comedies**
Favourite actors? **I like American actors**
What do you watch on television? **I hardly ever watch**
What is your favourite colour? **Red**
Favourite music? **Pop, rock, funk - disco music**
Favourite books? **I read the newspapers a bit but nothing else**
Your target in sport? **To continue to improve and to get to the top**
Beyond motor sport, who do you admire? **Apart from my family, I have never thought about it**
If you were left on a desert island, what would you take with you? **A kart, overalls and a helmet**
What is the most important thing in life for you? **My family and to be in good health**
What do you like most about your profession? **The driving and the fact that a racing team is like your second family**
What don't you like about your profession? **The relationship with the press. Certain journalists try to make you say what you don't want to say**
What are your principal strengths? **I don't know**
What are your faults? **I am too much of a perfectionist**
Have you thought about your retirement? **All in good time ...**

■ **PLUS POINTS:**

- Both drivers are experienced and quick
- Very professional team
- The Ferrari engine
- Reliability

■ **MINUS POINTS:**

- The departure of team manager Max Welti
- Located in Switzerland, far away from key English sub-contractors
- The economic crisis in south-east Asia, where main sponsor Petronas is based
- Team still suffers a degree of anonymity

Managing director:
Peter Sauber

Technical director:
Leo Ress

Address: Team Sauber Formel 1 AG,
Wildbachstrasse 9, 8340 Hinwil, Switzerland
Tel: 00 41 1938 14 00
Fax: 00 41 1983 16 80
Internet: www.redbull-sauber.ch.
Size of workforce: 150
First GP: South Africa 1993
**Number of Grands Prix: 81
0 wins, 0 pole positions**
Number of points scored: 80
Best result in world constructors' championship:
7th in 1993-95-1996-1997.
Best result in world drivers' championship:
9th in 1995 (H-H. Frentzen)
Test driver: Jörg Müller (Germany)

1997 result: 7th (16 points)

PETRONAS
Sauber

Petronas SPE 01D
Number of cylinders:
10 in 75deg vee
Capacity: 2998 cc
Power: 760 bhp
Weight: 120 kilos

Sauber C17 - Tyres: Goodyear

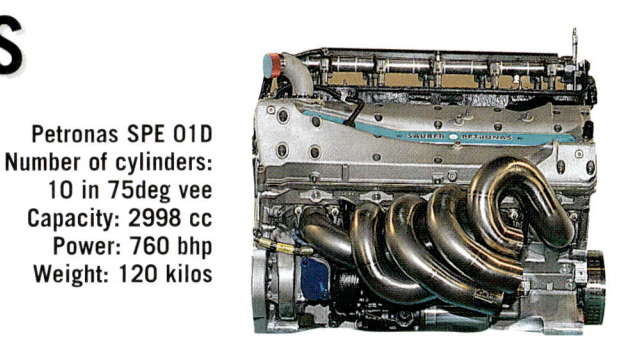

Peter Sauber chose the grandiose setting of the Schönbrunn orangery in Vienna to launch his team for 1998, as **Jean Alesi** joined to partner **Johnny Herbert**. They are currently the two most experienced drivers in F1. While some teams such as **Benetton** rush to sign up youth, **the Swiss team** is relying on the older brigade, not that this is necessarily a bad thing.
Alesi and **Herbert** rank among the quickest drivers in the field and they are both reliable finishers. The Swiss team is the hub of a cosmopolitan enterprise which features **a strong technical team**, the potent Ferrari engine (re-badged as a Petronas) and a healthy operating budget.
Sauber showed its hand straight away in Melbourne. **The effervescent Herbert** was disappointed only to finish sixth. **Alesi**, without much testing under his belt, was just starting to find his feet.

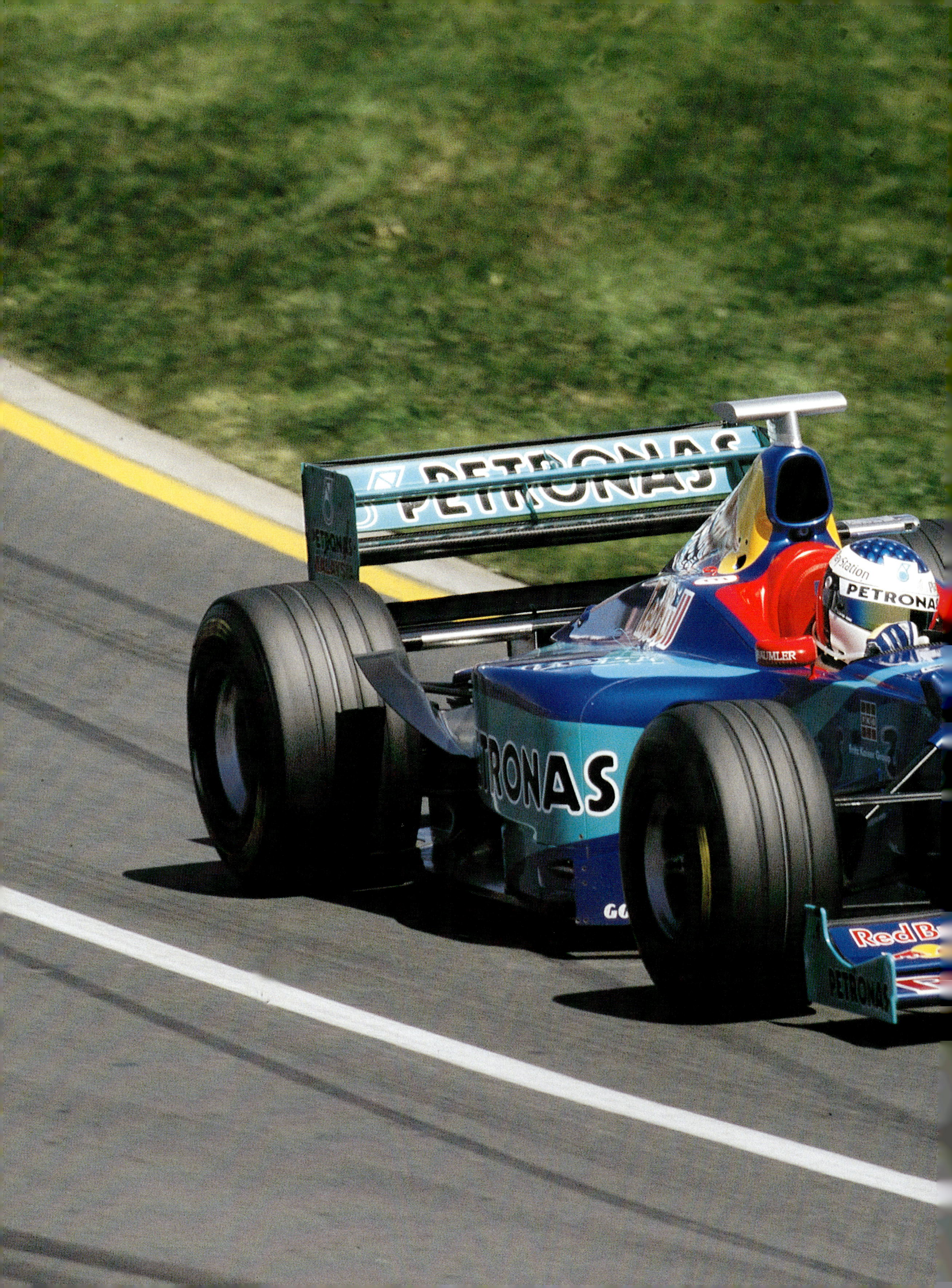
PETRONAS
PETRONAS

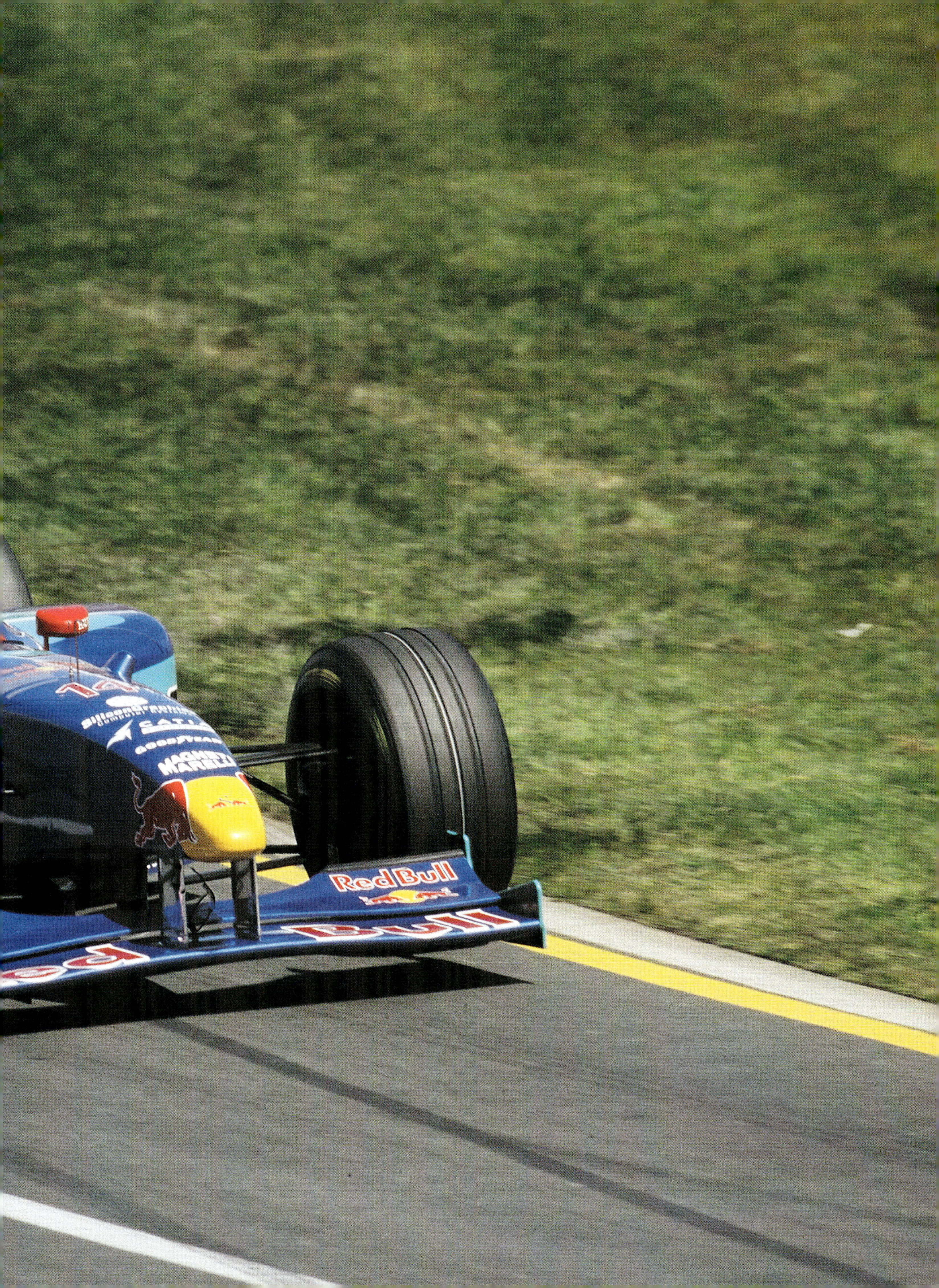
Red Bull
MAGNETI MARELLI

It was a huge surprise. The announcement that Jean Alesi was going to join Sauber caught the Formula One paddock unawares, since the whole world was waiting for an announcement that he would be teaming up again with his old friend Eddie Jordan. The Frenchman won the 1989 Formula 3000 title under Jordan's guidance, and had even lived in the same house for a while. Truly, Jean had been made a part of the family and everything augured well for a return to the Jordan fold. With the arrival of the Mugen-Honda engine, Jean was the ideal choice. But life is not always straightforward. Benson and Hedges, Jordan's tobacco sponsor, wanted to recruit Damon Hill as their driver no matter what the price. So, after negotiations with Peter Sauber at Hinwil, an agreement was swiftly reached. The Avignon driver has taken up a completely new challenge. At Benetton he suffered from the unrest caused in the wake of the departure of Schumacher and some of the brains behind his success, people such as Ross Brawn who had also left to join Ferrari. And with Flavio Briatore's farewell last summer, the soul of a winning team had gone. The Anglo-Italian team was no longer what it once was. Despite everything, Alesi had a good 1997 and finished on the podium several times. Unfortunately, the highest step was always beyond his reach. At Monza, victory escaped him only by a few extra fractions of a second taken during a refuelling stop. At Sauber he will join a well-drilled outfit which has a lot in its favour. Johnny Herbert, his new team-mate, will be a hard nut to crack. The British driver has already proved his speed and consistency. As one of the most spectacular drivers in the sport, the crowd-pleasing Jean should profit from the new tyre regulations introduced to make the racing safer and more exciting. He always drives with the bit between his teeth. And, what's more, he finds himself reunited with a Ferrari engine, albeit one which has been renamed for commercial reasons. In some ways, Alesi's move marks a return to his roots.

Team: Sauber - Petronas

Name:

Jean Alesi

Number 14

Date and place of birth: **11 June 1964, Avignon (France)**
Nationality: French
Place of residence: Geneva
Marital status: **Lives with Kumiko, two daughters, Charlotte and Elena**
Height and weight: **1.70 m / 70 kg**
First GP: French GP 1989 (Tyrrell)
Best position in world championship: 4th in 1996 and 1997 (Benetton)
135 GPs, 225 points, 1 win, 2 pole positions
French F3 champion in 1987
FIA F3000 champion in 1989
Record in F1: 1989: Tyrrell, 8 points, 9th in the championship,
1990: Tyrrell, 13 points, 9th, 1991: Ferrari, 21 points, 7th,
1992: Ferrari, 18 points, 7th, 1993: Ferrari, 16 points, 6th,
1994: Ferrari, 24 points, 5th, 1995: Ferrari, 42 points, 5th,
1996: Benetton, 47 points, 4th, 1997: Benetton, 36 points, 4th

Personal car? **M-class Mercedes … and a Fiat 500!**
Dream car? **None at the moment**
Favourite racing car? **The F3 Dallara of 1987 and the Tyrrell 018 of 1989**
Highlight of racing career? **Phoenix 1990 and my scuffle with Senna**
Worst moment of racing career? **Imola 1994**
Your favourite circuit? **Monza for the layout and the atmosphere**
Your least favourite circuit? **Budapest**
Your favourite driver of all time? **Alain Prost**
Your favourite current driver? **No one in particular**
Favourite food? **Pasta**
Favourite drink? **Fizzy water**
What sports do you take part in? **Weights, water skiing and jogging**
Favourite sports? **Team sports, particularly football, skiing and any sort of motor sports**
Favourite sportsmen? **Michael Jordan in basketball, Roberto Biaggio in football and Alberto Tomba**
Favourite type of film? **Action and adventure films**
Favourite actor and actress? **Mel Gibson and Sophie Marceau**
What do you watch on television? **Sport, the news and some documentaries**
What is your favourite colour? **Blue**
Favourite music? **Prince and light rock**
Favourite books? **Books on antiques, those about old watches or ancient architecture**
Your target in sport? **Passion comes before everything**
Beyond motor sport, who do you admire? **Winston Churchill and the great political figures of the Second World War fascinate me**
If you were left on a desert island, what would you take with you? **A gun so that I could blow my brains out!**
What is the most important thing in life for you? **My family and my health**
What do you like most about your profession? **The sensation of speed**
What don't you like about your profession? **I love all of it!**
What are your principal strengths? **Frankness and the ability to make a quick analysis of any situation**
What are your faults? **Frankness does not always please people!**
Have you thought about your retirement? **No**

It is rare not to see Johnny with a smile on his face. His mimicry and his facial expressions are almost as well known as those of Benny Hill or Mister Bean. This charming man is no less quick a driver for all that, and he has acquired a great deal of experience. He is about to embark on his third season with the Swiss team. Access to a Ferrari engine, rebadged as a Petronas in deference to a sponsor, has allowed him to challenge for points-scoring finishes. On the track his fighting spirit is not the least of his qualities. Last year he scored almost all of his team's points while his team-mates came and went. The reputation of Italians Larini and Morbidelli suffered by comparison. The young Argentinian Fontana was no match for an old campaigner who knows all the tricks of the trade. The arrival of Jean Alesi, another battle-hardened warrior, will increase Johnny's motivation tenfold. At Monaco in 1987, Johnny and Jean, then young F3 drivers, were together on the podium with race winner Didier Artzet, who has since retired. In the years which followed, both have plied their racecraft all over the world. The new regulations could well produce new challengers to the established hierarchy and Herbert is keen to give Sauber its first-ever Formula One success.

Team: Sauber - Petronas
Name:
Johnny Herbert
Number 15

Date and place of birth: **27 June 1964, Romford (England)**
Nationality: British
Place of residence: Monte Carlo
Marital status: **Married to Rebecca, two daughters, Amy and Chloe**
Height and weight: **1.67 m / 65 kg**
First GP: Brazilian GP 1989 (Benetton)
Best position in world championship: 4th in 1995 (Benetton)
112 GPs, 82 points, 2 wins, 0 pole positions
British F3 champion in 1987
Le Mans winner in 1991 (Mazda)
Record in F1: **1989: Benetton and Tyrrell: 0 points,**
1990 : Lotus: 0 points (2 GPs), 1991: Lotus: 0 points,
1992: Lotus: 2 points, 14th in the championship, 1993: Lotus: 11 points, 8th,
1994: Lotus, Ligier and Benetton: 0 points , 1995: Benetton: 45 points, 4th,
1996: Sauber: 4 points, 14th, 1997: Sauber: 15 points, 10th

Personal car? **A Ford Escort Cosworth and a Cherokee Jeep**
Dream car? **An Aston Martin DB7**
Favourite racing car? **The Benetton at the end of 1994 and the Lotus of 1992**
Highlight of racing career? **My victory at Silverstone in 1995 and my victory at Le Mans with Mazda in 1991**
Worst moment of racing career? **My F3000 accident at Brands Hatch in 1988**
Your favourite circuit? **Spa, it's a fabulous circuit**
Your least favourite circuit? **Hockenheim and Mount Fuji**
Your favourite driver of all time? **Gilles Villeneuve**
Your favourite current driver? **None in particular**
Favourite food? **Pasta**
Favourite drink? **Mineral water**
What sports do you take part in? **Golf, working out and cycling**
Favourite sports? **Golf**
Favourite sportsmen? **The decathlete Daley Thompson**
Favourite type of film? **Action movies and recently *The Full Monty***
Favourite actor/actress? **Buster Keaton and Sandra Bullock**
What do you watch on television? **A little of everything**
What is your favourite colour? **Orange**
Favourite music? **Chris Rea, Eric Clapton, The Eagles, Aerosmith and Stevie Winwood**
Favourite books? **Books about sport**
Your target in sport? **To be world champion**
Beyond motor sport, what do you admire? **The great humanitarian causes**
If you were left on a desert island, what would you take with you? **The most beautiful woman in the world …**
What is the most important thing in life for you? **My family and to be happy**
What do you like most about your profession? **The impression of speed and to do a perfect qualifying lap - what they call a flying lap!**
What don't you like about your profession? **Absolutely nothing**
What are your principal strengths? **That's not for me to say. That would be presumptuous**
What are your faults? **I'm too relaxed**
Have you thought about your retirement? **Certainly not**

■ **PLUS POINTS:**

- Tom Walkinshaw is a known winner
- The presence of proven designer John Barnard
- New TWR engine designed in collaboration with Brian Hart
- Diniz has maturity, Salo a hunger for success

■ **MINUS POINTS:**

- The departure of Damon Hill
- The absence of a mainstream technical partner
- Potential of the Arrows motor
- Late arrival of the A19 and of the new engine

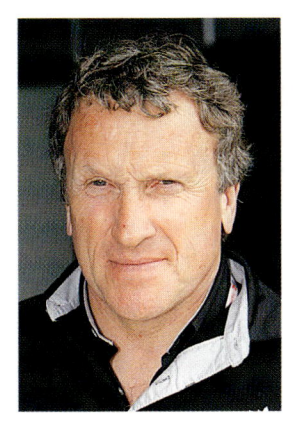

Managing director:
Tom Walkinshaw

Technical director:
John Barnard

Address: Arrows Grand Prix International Ltd
Leafield Technical Centre, Leafield
Witney, Oxon OX8 5PF, Great Britain
Tel: 00 44 1993 87 10 00
Fax: 00 44 1993 87 11 00
Internet: www.arrows.com
Size of workforce: 170
First GP: Brazil 1978
Number of Grands Prix: 305
Number of wins: 0
Number of pole positions: 1
Number of points scored: 150
Best result in world constructors' championship: 4th in 1988
Best result in world drivers' championship: 7th in 1988 (Warwick)
Test drivers: Emmanuel Collard (France) and Stephen Watson (South Africa)

1997 result: 9th (9 points)

TWR Arrows

Arrows A19 - Tyres: Bridgestone

Arrows-F1/V10
Number of cylinders: 10 in 72deg vee
Capacity: 2996 cc
Power: 740 bhp
Weight: 120 kilos

English designer **John Barnard's Arrows A19** is a good-looking car. Unfortunately, the Australian spectators did not get much of a look at it. Set back by myriad troubles since its very first test, it is still only at the developmental stage. For **the TWR-Arrows team**, the trip to the Antipodes was little more than a glorified test session. As narrow as it is innovative, **this splendid single-seater** needs to cover quite a few more kilometres before it is reliable. **Mika Salo** and **Pedro Diniz** need to be patient. Developed in partnership with **Brian Hart**, the **TWR V10 engine** is also too new to be ready for the heat of a Grand Prix battle. Nevertheless, one should have faith in **Tom Walkinshaw's team** achieving its objectives. A few months down the road and with a few thousand kilometres under its belt, the team will better be able to show its potential. The team owner, a stocky Scot with a passion for rugby, is not in F1 just to make up the numbers.

With his tanned complexion and hazel eyes, this handsome Brazilian is still working his way towards the top of the Formula One hierarchy. He made a low-key début in 1995 with the uncompetitive Forti team. Having served his apprenticeship, he moved on the following year to Ligier, where sometimes he was able to rattle team-mate Olivier Panis. An even better barometer of his progress came at Arrows in 1997, where he shared a pit garage with reigning world champion Damon Hill. He was never embarrassed by his illustrious team leader. With the continued support of his faithful sponsors, he is staying on at Arrows and is determined to further his career. The presence of new team-mate Mika Salo will be excellent motivation. A true gentleman, always smiling and available, Pedro is one of the most engaging drivers in the pit lane. Last year, Williams's technical director Patrick Head told a group of journalists that the Brazilian was the revelation of the season. He can only draw encouragement from such a glowing tribute.

Team : TWR - Arrows

Name :

Pedro Diniz

Number 16

Date and place of birth: **22 May 1970, São Paulo (Brazil)**
Nationality: Brazilian
Places of residence: Monte Carlo and São Paulo
Marital status: **Single**
Height and weight: **1.74 m / 69 kg**
First GP: **Brazilian GP 1995 (Forti)**
Best position in world championship: 15th in 1996 (Ligier)
50 GPs, 4 points
Record in F1: **1995: Forti 0 points,**
1996: Ligier 2 points, 15th in the championship,
1997: Arrows 2 points, 16th

Personal car? **Volvo 670**
Dream car? **Ferrari 550**
Favourite racing car? **The Ligier of 1996**
Highlight of racing career? **My 5th place at the Nürburgring in 1997 and also at Spa where I was 3rd for a while.**
Worst moment of racing career? **An accident in F3 in 1991.**
I had some broken vertebrae
Your favourite circuit? **Barcelona**
Your least favourite circuit? **None in particular**
Your favourite driver of all time? **Ayrton Senna**
Your favourite current driver? **Michael Schumacher**
Favourite food? **Pasta, spaghetti in particular**
Favourite drink? **Mineral water**
What sports do you take part in? **Cycling, jogging, cross-country skiing, water skiing, jet-skiing and squash**
Favourite sport? **Tennis**
Favourite sportsmen? **Michael Jordan**
Favourite type of film? **Action films. I recently enjoyed** *The Devil's Advocate* **and** *Titanic*
Favourite actress? **I like Julia Roberts a lot**
What do you watch on television? **I hardly ever watch television, it bores me**
What is your favourite colour? **Blue**
Favourite music? **Sade and light rock, and the Brazilian bosanova**
Favourite books? **Good thrillers**
Your target in sport? **To enjoy myself**
Beyond motor sport, who do you admire? **High-risk sportsmen**
If you were left on a desert island, what would you take with you? **A beautiful woman**
What is the most important thing in life for you? **To be happy**
What do you like most about your profession? **Driving motor cars**
What don't you like about your profession? **The pressure**
What are your principal strengths? **On the track it's speed**
What are your faults? **Sometimes I'm too impulsive**
Have you thought about retirement? **No, not yet!**

The 1990 British F3 Championship was dominated by a brace of young Finns. The two Mikas obliterated the opposition. Runner-up that year to Mika Hakkinen, Mika Salo also has a promising future. While his compatriot moved straight into F1, Salo chose to go to Japan. In 1994 he made his Formula One début at Suzuka with Lotus, which was on the verge of collapse. Taken on the following year by the wily Ken Tyrrell, he became the spearhead of the English team. Unfortunately times were hard for this venerable British outfit. Poor Mika never had the means to compete on equal terms with the opposition. Nevertheless he has often picked up a few points, much to Tyrrell's delight. His transfer to the well-structured Arrows team will give him a chance to get his hands on good equipment and should signal the dawn of a new era. F1's second blond Finn has certainly not yet earned the reputation of his compatriot Hakkinen, but he doesn't intend to remain forever in his shadow. Of course, his Arrows is no McLaren, but it ought to allow him to have his big day. Mika Salo is a surefire talent. A great friend of Jacques Villeneuve, he is impatient to be able to tussle with him on the circuit - as well as on skidoos in the north of Finland - to demonstrate his true worth to a wider audience. His performances have already attracted the attention of a number of top teams, and paddock gossips frequently predict that Ferrari will snap him up. Calm, always smiling, this well educated young man is waiting for his moment.

Team : TWR - Arrows

Number 17

Name : Mika Salo

Date and place of birth: **30 November 1966, Helsinki (Finland)**
Nationality: Finnish
Place of residence: London
Marital status: Single
Height and weight: **1.75 m / 65 kg**
First GP: Japanese GP 1994 (Lotus)
Best position in world championship: **13th in 1996 (Tyrrell)**
52 GPs, 12 points, 0 wins, 0 pole positions
Record in F1: **1994: Lotus (2 GPs), 0 point,
1995: Tyrrell: 5 points, 14th in the championship,
1996: Tyrrell: 5 points, 13th, 1997: Tyrrell: 2 points, 16th**

Personal car? **I've several but mostly I drive a Volvo 670**
Dream car? **A car with lots of room which goes very fast!**
Favourite racing car? **I hope it will be the 1998 Arrows!**
Highlight of racing career? **My first F1 race in Japan in a Lotus, which I managed to keep and which is now at my home in Finland**
Worst moment of racing career? **I actually can't think of any**
Your favourite circuit? **Suzuka**
Your least favourite circuit? **Mount Fuji**
Your favourite driver of all time? **James Hunt**
Your favourite current driver? **I don't have any**
Favourite food? **Pasta**
Favourite drink? **Milk**
What sports do you take part in? **Skidooing when I'm in Finland. Apart from that, jogging, gym work and cycling**
Favourite sports? **I love snowboarding competitions**
Favourite sportsmen? **An ice hockey player, Teemu Selanne who plays for the Anaheim Ducks**
Favourite type of film? **Action movies, comedies and recently** *Titanic*
Favourite actors/actresses? **Meg Ryan and comedy actors. I like all actresses ...**
What do you watch on television? **I love channel-surfing**
What is your favourite colour? **Blue**
What is your favourite music? **Heavy rock, I have thousands of CDs**
Favourite books? **Comic strips**
Your target in sport? **To enjoy myself as a driver**
Beyond motor sport, who do you admire? **There are too many people to make a list**
If you were left on a desert island, what would you take with you? **Lots to eat!**
What is the most important thing in life for you? **My health**
What do you like most about your profession? **The freedom**
What don't you like about your profession? **Sitting in planes**
What are your principal strengths? **That's not for me to say, that would be presumptuous**
What are your faults? **Lots of nasty things**
Have you thought about your retirement? **No, I'm still too young, let me live a little first**

■ **PLUS POINTS:**

- Strong support from Ford
- New engine should be more reliable
- Experience and motivation of Barrichello
- Team has completed its apprenticeship

■ **MINUS POINTS:**

- The solidity of the budget?
- Ford engine reliability last year
- Pressure from Ford

President:
Jackie Stewart

Technical director:
Alan Jenkins

Address: Stewart Grand Prix Ltd,
16 Tanners Drive, Blakelands, Milton Keynes,
Bucks MK14 5BW, Great Britain.
Tel: 00 44 1908 21 51 00
Fax: 00 44 1908 21 68 92
Internet: n/a
Managing director: Paul Stewart
Size of workforce: 136
First GP: Australia 1997
Number of Grands Prix: 17
0 wins, 0 pole positions
Number of points scored: 6
Best result in world constructors' championship: 9th in 1997
Best result in world drivers' championship: Barrichello, 14th in 1997

1997 result: 9th (6 points)

FORD *Stewart*

Ford Zetec-R V10
Number of cylinders:
10 in 72deg vee
Capacity: 2998 cc
Power: 750 bhp
Weight: 120 kilos

Stewart SF-2 - Tyres: Bridgestone

Rubens Barrichello's second place in Monaco was the highlight of a first season marred by an interminable series of engine failures. This year, **the Stewart team** is determined to set the record straight. Launched early in January, **the Stewart SF-02** should have started the year with thousands of kilometres under its belt. Unfortunately, the carbon gearbox casing shattered the team's hopes. As with **Arrows**, the early tests were difficult. With reliability in short supply, the Stewart spent its days in the shadow of the pit lane. While waiting for things to pick up, **Rubens Barrichello** and **Jan Magnussen** could only sit and watch as their rivals sped by.
But extra input from Ford, a decent budget and a strengthened workforce should eventually lead to improved performances from a team with **a strong flavour of Scotland**.

Known affectionately as Rubinho ('little Rubens'), this Brazilian was born within a few hundred metres of the Interlagos circuit. His countrymen consider him to be the heir to the late, great Ayrton Senna, whose helmet colours he wore by way of tribute during his home Grand Prix in 1995. Despite showing flashes of promise he has yet to live up to those expectations. But then again, the Jordan he previously had at his disposal was hardly in the McLaren class.

The creation of the Stewart team last year gave Barrichello the opportunity to polish his reputation. At Monaco he was the only driver able to challenge the furious pace of the Ferraris in a torrential downpour. His second place was a remarkable achievement. He often qualified well only to be let down by the unreliability of the Ford engine. After an alarming sequence of smoky failures, the Detroit giant is looking to put things right. Nicknamed 'Popeye' by some, Rubens must make the most of his current situation if he is ever to earn his place in the limelight. He has the talent, the experience and the potential to fulfil his ambitions. Like his compatriot Ronaldo, who came to watch him last year in Barcelona, he could carry the Brazilian colours right to the very top.

Team: Stewart - Ford
Name: Rubens Barrichello
Number 18

Date and place of birth: **23 May 1972, São Paulo (Brazil)**
Nationality: **Brazilian**
Place of residence: **Monte Carlo**
Marital status: **Married to Silvana**
Height and weight: **1.72 m / 79 kg**
First GP: **South African GP 1993 (Jordan)**
Best position in world championship: **6th in 1994 (Jordan)**
81 GPs, 52 points, 0 wins, 1 pole position
Opel Lotus Euroseries champion in 1990
British F3 champion in 1991
Record in F1: **1993: Jordan, 2 points, 17th in the championship, 1994: Jordan, 19 points, 6th, 1995: Jordan, 11 points, 11th, 1996: Jordan, 14 points, 8th, 1997: Stewart, 6 points, 14th**

Personal car? **Ford Explorer V8**
Dream car? **Ferrari**
Favourite racing car? **The 1994 Jordan and the 1997 Stewart**
Highlight of racing career? **My second place at Monaco in 1997**
Worst moment of racing career? **Imola 1994**
Your favourite circuit? **Interlagos, it's my back yard!**
Your least favourite circuit? **None, every track has its charm.**
Your favourite driver of all time? **Ayrton Senna**
Your favourite current driver? **None**
Favourite food? **Pasta**
Favourite drink? **Pepsi light**
What sports do you take part in? **Jogging, squash and tennis**
Favourite sports? **Football, jet skiing and motor racing**
Favourite sportsmen? **Pete Sampras, Ronaldo and always Ayrton Senna**
Favourite type of film? **Any film with Robert de Niro, and right now** *Titanic*
Favourite actors/actresses? **Julia Roberts, Sandra Bullock and Robert de Niro**
What do you watch on television? **Anything entertaining**
What is your favourite colour? **Blue**
Favourite music? **Brazilian groups, but not heavy rock, Laura Pasolini and Eros Ramazzotti**
Favourite books? **Sports magazines**
Your target in sport? **To become world champion**
Beyond motor sport, who do you admire? **My father and my family**
If you were left on a desert island, what would you take with you? **My wife Silvana**
What is the most important thing in life for you? **To be happy**
What do you like most about your profession? **The impression of speed and to win**
What don't you like about your profession? **The politics**
What are your principal strengths? **I am my own man**
What are your faults? **Not coping better with pressure**
Have you thought about your retirement? **To go IndyCar racing in the States and to live in Miami**

In 1994 the British Formula 3 Championship was dominated by the 21-year-old Dane. He won 14 out of 18 races. It was an even better record than Ayrton Senna's 11 years earlier, and it was logical that Magnussen should be christened as the next Senna. The young prodigy became a test driver for McLaren and competed in the Pacific Grand Prix, where he finished 11th. Under the patronage of Mercedes, he took part in the German Touring Car Championship - the famous DTM which was transformed into the International Touring Car Championship prior to its demise. To complete his apprenticeship, he crossed the Atlantic to compete in four IndyCar races with the Penske team. Jan the Viking was ready to make the big leap and his partnership with the Stewart team has given him the chance to achieve his objective. The famous racing Stewarts, who brought him to prominence in F3, are giving him the chance to learn the Grand Prix driver's art without undue pressure. Even so, 1997 was a difficult year for him. Bothered by mechanical problems and inexperienced, he was a shadow of his former self. In testing his times were a long way shy of those of his team-mate, Barrichello, and things were no better at the races.

Then, little by little, he rediscovered his resolve and made up for his slow start, despite the fragility of the Ford engine. Towards the end of the season he put in some excellent qualifying performances. Paul and Jackie Stewart, who know him well, have kept their faith in him. The laborious apprenticeship is now over and Magnussen must become a regular points-scorer and make the most of this chance to show his mettle. It's double or quits. There is no place for philanthropy in Formula One.

Team: **Stewart - Ford**

Name: **Jan Magnussen**

Number **19**

Date and place of birth: **4 July 1973, Roskilde (Denmark)**
Nationality: **Danish**
Place of residence: **Silverstone (England)**
Marital status: **Single, son Kevin**
Height and weight: **1.70 m / 58 kg**
First GP: **Pacific GP 1995 (McLaren)**
Best position in world championship: **Unclassified**
18 GPs, 0 points , 0 wins, 0 pole positions
British F3 champion in 1994
Record in F1: **1995: McLaren (1 GP), 0 points,**
1997: Stewart:, 0 points

Personal car? **A Ford Explorer V6**
Dream car? **The McLaren F1 road car**
Favourite racing car? **Formula One and IndyCar single-seaters**
Highlight of racing career? **Macau F3 in 1994**
Worst moment of racing career? **The whole 1997 F1 season!**
Your favourite circuit? **Road America at Indy and Spa**
Your least favourite circuit? **The Helsinki track in the ITC**
Your favourite driver of all time? **Ayrton Senna**
Your favourite current driver? **None**
Favourite food? **A Big Mac, occasionally, and health food**
Favourite drink? **Anything refreshing**
What sports do you take part in? **Shooting, jogging, karting and gym work**
Favourite sports? **Alpine skiing, in particular downhill and slalom**
Favourite sportsmen? **Mike Tyson and Michael Johnson**
Favourite type of film? **Action films, I loved *Titanic*, and the films of Quentin Tarantino**
Favourite actor/actress? **Harrison Ford and Meg Ryan**
What do you watch on television? **A little of everything**
What is your favourite colour? **Blue**
Favourite music? **Dance music as well as heavy rock**
Favourite books? **Science fiction**
Your target in sport? **To be successful and to be world champion**
Beyond motor sport, who do you admire? **My son**
If you were left on a desert island, what would you take with you? **Some good books and ... perhaps Claudia Schiffer!**
What is the most important thing in life for you? **My son and my family**
What do you like most about your profession? **The rush of adrenaline, the sensation and the concentration**
What don't you like about your profession? **There is too much work and too much pressure**
What are your principal strengths? **Honesty**
What are your faults? **I'm too self-indulgent. For example, when I am enjoying myself with my son I know I should be working or training**
Have you thought about your retirement? **No, not yet**

PLUS POINTS:

- Takeover by BAT
- Financial stability
- Ford V10 is a step up from last year's V8

MINUS POINTS:

- Departure of Ken Tyrrell
- The complete inexperience of the Japanese driver Takagi
- Lack of experience of Rosset
- The absence of a mainstream technical partner
- Loss of motivation from parts of the team that will not be kept on when the team moves to British American Racing's new HQ?

Managing director:
Craig Pollock

Technical director:
Harvey Postlethwaite

Address: Tyrrell Racing Organisation
Long Beach, Ockham, Woking, Surrey
GU23 6PE, Great Britain.
Tel: 00 44 1483 28 49 55
Fax: 00 44 1483 28 48 92
Internet: www.tyrrellF1.com
Size of workforce: 117
First GP: South Africa 1968 (Matra) and Canada 1970 (Tyrrell)
Number of Grands Prix: 402
Number of wins: 33 (9 with Matra and 1 with March)
Number of pole positions: 14 (Tyrrell)
Number of points scored: 615 (Tyrrell)
World constructors' titles: 1 in 1971
World drivers' titles: 3 (J. Stewart in 1969-71-73)
Test driver: Jean-Christophe Boullion (France)

1997 result: 10th (2 points)

BAR FORD Tyrrell

BAR-Tyrrell-Ford - Tyres: Goodyear

Ford Zetec-R V10 (Client version)
Number of cylinders:
10 in 72deg vee
Capacity: 2998 cc
Power: 735 bhp
Weight: 125 kilos

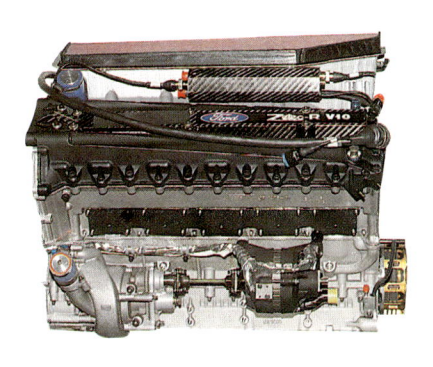

Following its acquisition by **British American Racing**, this marks the final season of **the legendary Tyrrell team** in its original form. The sudden departure of **Ken Tyrrell**, founding father of one of the pillars of F1, caused a pre-season stir at a team which is now managed by **Craig Pollock**. At the root of the split was a difference of opinion over who **Takagi's team-mate** should be. **The veteran Ken** had wanted to bow out on a high. The **026**, the last car produced under his control, looks to have great promise and for once has a half-decent engine. Despite his total lack of F1 experience, **young Takagi** has been upsetting the form book, working his way in front of the Jordans, for instance. Throughout the season, **the spirited young Japanese** looks set to fly the flag as the Tyrrell days draw to a close. Will **Ken Tyrrell** be able to resist the temptation to come and watch his cars before it is too late?

On 21 January, the day of the unveiling in London of the Tyrrell 026, people learnt with amazement that the team-mate for Takagi was still not known. There was no lack of applicants for the last driving slot for the new season. Verstappen, Marques, Boullion and Fontana were still hopeful up to the last minute. Ricardo Rosset, the 29-year-old Brazilian pipped his worthy rivals on the post, thanks it has to be said to some staunch supporters. After an impressive season in Formula 3000 in 1995 where he finished runner-up to Sospiri, he began his F1 career with Arrows in 1996 on the crest of a wave. Taken on by Tom Walkinshaw in mid-season, he never had the chance to show his true worth with a car that underperformed. The brief adventure with Lola, which ended after the first Grand Prix of last year, plunged him into the misery of unemployment. He might have been lost to Formula One but Tyrrell has given him the opportunity to bounce back. The well-conceived Tyrrell 026 is the surprise of the winter's work. After a full year of inactivity, Ricardo must now get back into the swing of things and rediscover his form. A healthy and competitive car is a sure way to reveal to the public this rather reserved but very likeable young man.

Team: **Tyrrell - BAR - Ford**

Name: **Ricardo Rosset**

Number **20**

Date and place of birth: **27 July 1968, São Paulo (Brazil)**
Nationality: Brazilian
Places of residence: Cambridge (England) and São Paulo (Brazil)
Marital status: **Engaged to Michelle**
Height and weight: **1.74 m / 67 kg**
First GP: **Brazilian GP 1996 (Arrows)**
Best position in world championship: **Unclassified**
16 GPs, 0 points, 0 wins, 0 pole positions
Record in F1: **1996: Arrows, 0 points**

Personal car? **Mercedes C36**
Dream car? **Ferrari 355**
Favourite racing car? **The car that will help me win. My dream is to drive a Ferrari**
Highlight of racing career? **My first karting victory in Brazil and my F3000 season in 1995**
Worst moment of racing career? **The farce with Lola in 1997**
Your favourite circuit? **The long fast circuits like Spa and Barcelona**
Your least favourite circuit? **Budapest and Buenos Aires**
Your favourite driver of all time? **Ayrton Senna**
Your favourite current driver? **My friend Rubens Barrichello**
Favourite food? **Pasta and Italian cooking**
Favourite drink? **A good glass of red wine from time to time**
What sports do you take part in? **Jogging, cycling, tennis and water skiing**
Favourite sports? **All motor sports, cycling, alpine skiing and diving**
Favourite sportsmen? **Michael Johnson and Ronaldo**
Favourite type of film? **Action films**
Favourite actors/actresses? **Robert Redford, Mel Gibson, Sandra Bullock, Sharon Stone and Demi Moore**
What do you watch on television? **Sport, news and documentaries**
What is your favourite colour? **Blue**
Favourite music? **Phil Collins and Brazilian pop music**
Favourite books? **I don't like reading**
Your target in sport? **To reach the top, to win races and then become champion**
Beyond motor sport, who do you admire? **My father**
If you were left on a desert island, what would you take with you? **Michelle, my fiancée**
What is the most important thing in life for you? **To be happy and healthy**
What do you like most about your profession? **The technology and the constant challenge**
What don't you like about your profession? **Getting up too early!**
What are your principal strengths? **Perseverance and stubbornness**
What are your faults? **These qualities are also faults**
Have you thought about your retirement? **I have a sports clothes company in Brazil called Track and Field**

The prodigy of former racer Satoru Nakajima, who had a solid career in Europe during the Eighties thanks to support from Honda, 24-year-old Tora Takagi is coming to have a crack at Formula One. He competed for the Nakajima Planning team in Formula Nippon, the Japanese equivalent of F3000, taking six race wins and a dozen pole positions. He is very quick, but his sense of adventure can sometimes get the better of him. When Nakajima decided to assist his protégé to the top level of motor sport, he enlisted the help of a trusty sponsor and signed a contract with Ken Tyrrell to make a seat available. Takagi was named as test driver and was certain to graduate to the race team the following year. And that was that. Thanks to a cast-iron contract, and despite the takeover of the team by BAT, this deal will be honoured. Throughout the whole of last season he took part in many of Tyrrell's private test sessions. In order to help him get to know the circuits, he was signed up to take part in some Porsche Cup events and he returned frequently to Japan to compete in Formula Nippon. Tora Takagi has the means to do well. He is ambitious, has some good people around him and his new team has played an important role in developing young drivers. The only problem will be acclimatising to European life, which is never easy for those from the Land of the Rising Sun. The barriers of language, culture, food, way of life and different mentalities are all hurdles which have to be faced. Shinji Nakano could tell him a bit about that.

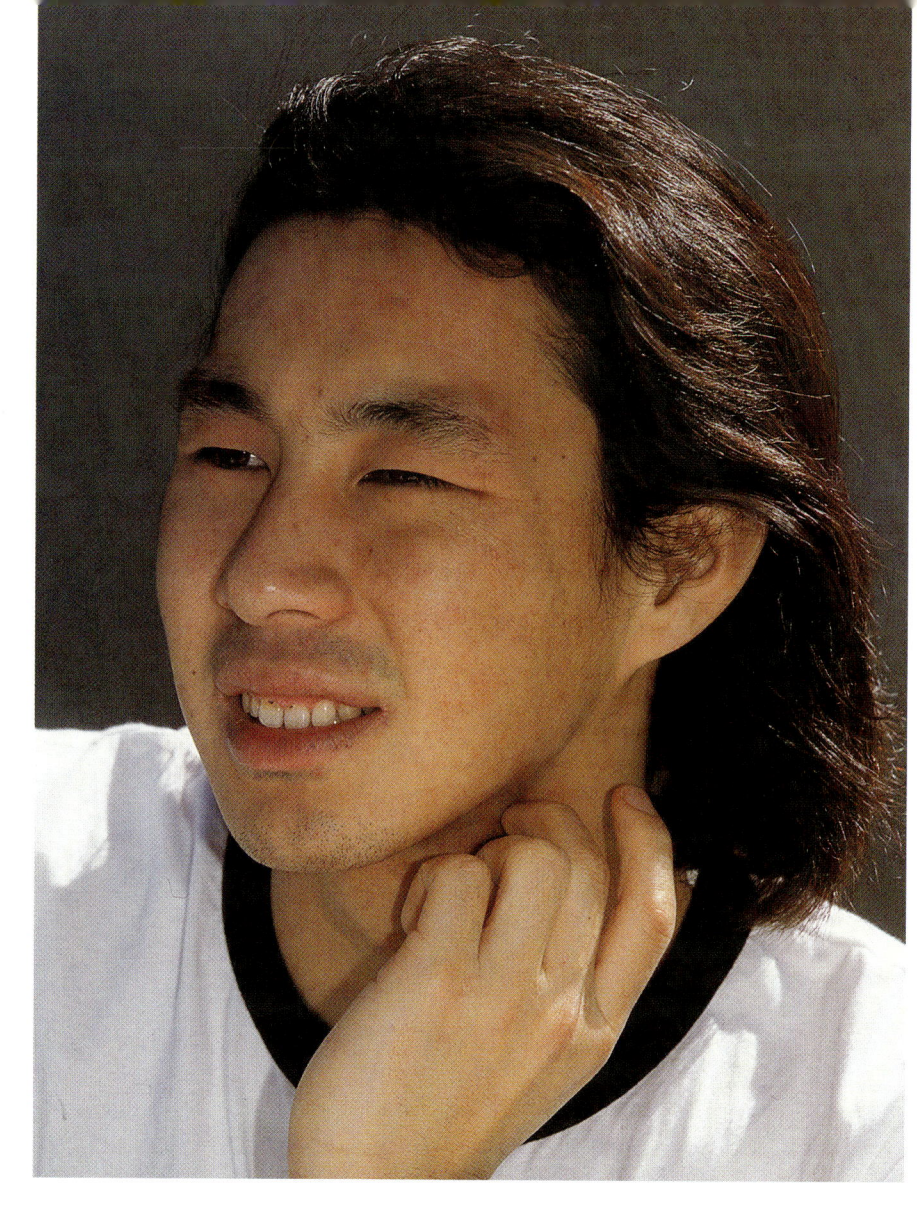

Team: Tyrrell - BAR - Ford

Number 21

Name: Toranosuke Takagi

Date and place of birth: **12 February 1974, Shizuoka (Japan)**
Nationality: Japanese
Place of residence: London
Marital status: Single
Height and weight: **1.80 m / 61 kg**
First year in F1

Personal car? **A Honda Shuttle**
Dream car? **Such a car does not exist!**
Favourite racing car? **The 1998 Tyrrell 026**
Highlight of racing career? **I am not the sort of person to store such memories**
Worst moment of racing career? **All my retirements**
Your favourite circuit? **Suzuka**
Your least favourite circuit? **The circuits where I would have no hope of winning**
Your favourite driver of all time? **I try not to dream about such things**
Your favourite current driver? **No one**
Favourite food? **Italian pasta**
Favourite drink? **Sparkling mineral water**
What sports do you take part in? **Snowboarding (Sh! … it's against team rules!)**
Favourite sports? **None in particular**
Favourite sportsmen? **No one**
Favourite type of film? **I always watch all the films on the long flights between Japan and Europe**
Favourite actor? **None in particular**
What do you watch on television? **In Japan I like the comedy programmes**
What is your favourite colour? **Green, which is also the colour of my helmet**
Favourite music? **Pop music and especially Japanese rock**
Favourite books? **I don't enjoy reading**
Your target in sport? **To always do my best**
Beyond motor sport, who do you admire? **Lots of people in all walks of life**
If you were left on a desert island, what would you take with you? **I don't want to even think about it**
What is the most important thing in life for you? **That's life!**
What do you like most about your profession? **The thrill of driving**
What don't you like about your profession? **Having to appear in public. I like to be on my own.**
What are your principal strengths? **I'm very determined**
What are your faults? **I'm too determined**
Have you thought about your retirement? **I never think about it!**

PLUS POINTS:

- Good financial situation
- The will to succeed
- Dynamism of technical partner Fondmetal
- Arrival of Gustav Brunner

MINUS POINTS:

- The complete inexperience of Tuero who is only 19!
- Drivers chosen for their sponsorship, not for their experience
- Performance of customer Ford V10

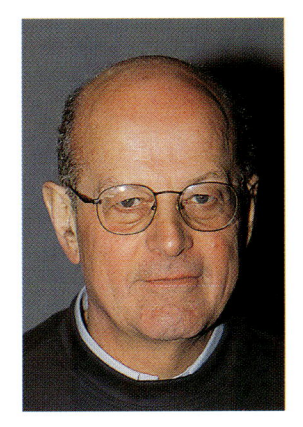

President: **Gabriele Rumi**

Technical director: **Gustav Brunner**

Address: Minardi Team Spa,
Via Spallanzani 21,
48 018 Faenza (Ra), Italy
Tel: 00 39 546 620 480
Fax: 00 39 546 620 998
Internet: www.minardi.it
Managing director: Giancarlo Minardi
Size of workforce: 90
First GP: Brazil 1985
Number of Grands Prix: 205
0 wins, 0 pole positions
Number of points scored: 27
Best result in world constructors' championship: 7th in 1991
Best result in world drivers' championship: 7th in 1991 (Martini)
Test driver: Laurent Redon (France)

1997 result: 0 points

FORD Minardi

Ford Zetec-R V10
(Client version)
Number of cylinders:
10 in 72deg vee
Capacity: 2998 cc
Power: 735 bhp
Weight: 125 kilos

Minardi M198 - Tyres: Bridgestone

Fondmetal president **Gabriele Rumi** is now the majority shareholder at Minardi. He and his friend **Gian Carlo Minardi** have decided to take the bull by the horns.
Gustav Brunner has quit the Ferrari design studio and has rejoined **the Faenza team**. And its more famous neighbour wasn't happy about it. But despite considerable pressure, Rumi got his man. Drivers **Nakano** and **Tuero** arrived accompanied by no shortage of dollars. A decent **Ford V10** could allow Italy's 'other' team to progress.
While **Tuero** remains something of an unknown quantity, **Shinji Nakano** is desperate to prove a point, and would love to make **Prost** regret its decision to let him go. Now well structured, **Minardi is ambitious** and wants to step up a gear.

It looked as though Shinji Nakano was about to be lost to Formula One. His Honda connections had helped him find a seat at Ligier for 1997, but then the team was taken over by Alain Prost. The young Japanese protégé's career prospects with the new French team looked slim and confirmation of Prost's 1998 deal with Peugeot left him in the wilderness.

Honda's influence enabled 'Nakanosan' to hold on to his place in the team last year, but it was difficult for him to keep up his spirits when he knew he was on the way out. Nevertheless, he managed to get into the points and he drove some good races despite difficult circumstances. As expected, he was thanked then cast adrift immediately after Jerez and it looked as though this pleasant young man would never reappear in the Grand Prix jungle. However, thanks to backing from a loyal sponsor he managed to secure one of the last available seats for this season. The restructured Minardi team could present Shinji with some interesting opportunities. Victories certainly won't be on his mind but he will be determined to prove that the team's confidence in him was not misplaced.

Team: Minardi - Ford

Name: Shinji Nakano

Number 22

Date and place of birth: **1 April 1971, Osaka (Japan)**
Nationality: Japanese
Place of residence: Faenza (Italy)
Marital status: **Single**
Height and weight: **1.74 m / 63 kg**
First GP: Australian GP 1997 (Prost)
Best position in world championship:
18th in 1997 (Prost)
17 GPs, 2 points, 0 wins, 0 pole positions
Record in F1: **1997: Prost, 2 points, 18th in the championship**

Personal car? **A Ford Escort**
Dream car? **None in particular**
Favourite racing car? **The Dome F1**
Highlight of racing career? **The 1997 British Grand Prix, even though I had to retire**
Worst moment of racing career? **In 1992 I was racing in F3 and F3000 at the same time: there were too many problems and too much pressure**
Your favourite circuit? **Suzuka and Silverstone**
Your least favourite circuit? **Imola**
Your favourite driver of all time? **None really**
Your favourite current driver? **None in particular**
Favourite food? **Japanese, Italian and French food**
Favourite drink? **Water and milk.**
What sports do you take part in? **Golf, tennis, squash, karting and occasionally skiing**
Favourite sports? **I'm not a great follower of any sport**
Favourite sportsmen? **None**
Favourite type of film? **I like action films most**
Favourite actors? **That's difficult to answer**
What do you watch on television? **Films and a bit of Eurosport**
What is your favourite colour? **Blue and black**
Favourite music? **All types of music except hard rock**
Favourite books? **Books on Japanese history**
Your target in sport? **To realise my dream**
Beyond motor sport, who do you admire? **Nobody in particular**
If you were left on a desert island, what would you take with you? **I wouldn't dare to imagine such a disaster**
What is the most important thing in life for you? **To remain a Formula One driver**
What do you like most about your profession? **Driving and above all winning**
What don't you like about your profession? **There are too many people involved. There's too much politics in the sport.**
What are your principal strengths? **I can't answer that**
What are your faults? **I'm saying nothing!**
Have you thought about your retirement? **Not yet**

On 8 March 1998, the day of the Australian Grand Prix, this young Argentinian with the looks of a toreador will become the third youngest driver in Formula One history, after Mike Thackwell and Ricardo Rodriguez, beginning his career at 19 years, 10 months and 14 days.
Spotted in Formula 2000 by Gian Carlo Minardi in 1995, when he started five races in Italy, won them all and also took the championship, he now becomes a Minardi driver. After a few races in F3 and a front row start in Monaco alongside Trulli in 1996, he became test driver for Minardi. Last year he tried his luck without success in Formula 3000 in Japan. With the backing of a whole nation, he found the money needed to secure his place in F1. Paradoxically, his compatriot Fontana failed to arouse the same feeling in the country. All the tickets for the 1998 Argentinian GP carry the face of young Esteban. It is an amazing popular reaction. An enormous poster campaign is planned for him in Buenos Aires. The Argentinians consider him to be the natural successor to Fangio, Gonzalez and Reutemann. In a much reorganised Minardi team, young Tuero will learn his trade without pressure and will wait for his time to come.

Team : Minardi - Ford

Number **23**

Name : **Esteban Tuero**

Date and place of birth: **22 April 1978, Buenos Aires (Argentina)**
Nationality: **Argentinian**
Places of residence: **Buenos Aires (Argentina) and Faenza (Italy)**
Marital status: **Single**
Height and weight: **1.67 m / 66 kg**
Argentinian Formula Honda champion in 1994
Italian F2000 champion in 1995
First year in F1

Personal car? **Honda Accord**
Dream car? **A Ferrari**
Favourite racing car? **The 1996 F3 Dallara and also the Minardi!**
Highlight of racing career? **To be on the front line of the grid with Trulli in the Monaco F3 race in 1996**
Worst moment of racing career? **I haven't had one**
Your favourite circuit? **Monaco and Buenos Aires**
Your least favourite circuit? **I don't have one**
Your favourite driver of all time? **Fangio, Gonzalez, Senna, Prost and Mansell**
Your favourite current driver? **Michael Schumacher and Fisichella**
Favourite food? **L'asado, a meat dish from Argentina**
Favourite drink? **Fresh orange juice**
What sports do you take part in? **Football and squash**
Favourite sports? **Following the Argentina football team and tennis**
Favourite sportsmen? **Football players - Maradonna, Gallardo, Ortega and Battistutta**
What do you watch on television? **Detective thrillers**
Favourite actors? **Al Pacino among others**
What do you watch on television? **A little of everything and nothing in particular**
What is your favourite colour? **Sky blue and white, the Argentinian colours**
Favourite music? **Light rock, the Eagles …**
Favourite books? **I don't read much, sometimes the newspapers**
Your target in sport? **To give my best, the very most**
Beyond motor sport, who do you admire? **No one really**
If you were left on a desert island, what would you take with you? **A beautiful girl**
What is the most important thing in life for you? **My family and to do what I want to do**
What do you like most about your profession? **The professionalism**
What don't you like about your profession? **The people, and there are lots of them, who speak without knowing what they are talking about**
What are your principal strengths? **I like to learn**
What are your faults? **I don't know!**
Have you thought about your retirement? **That'll depend on the money that I might have earned …**

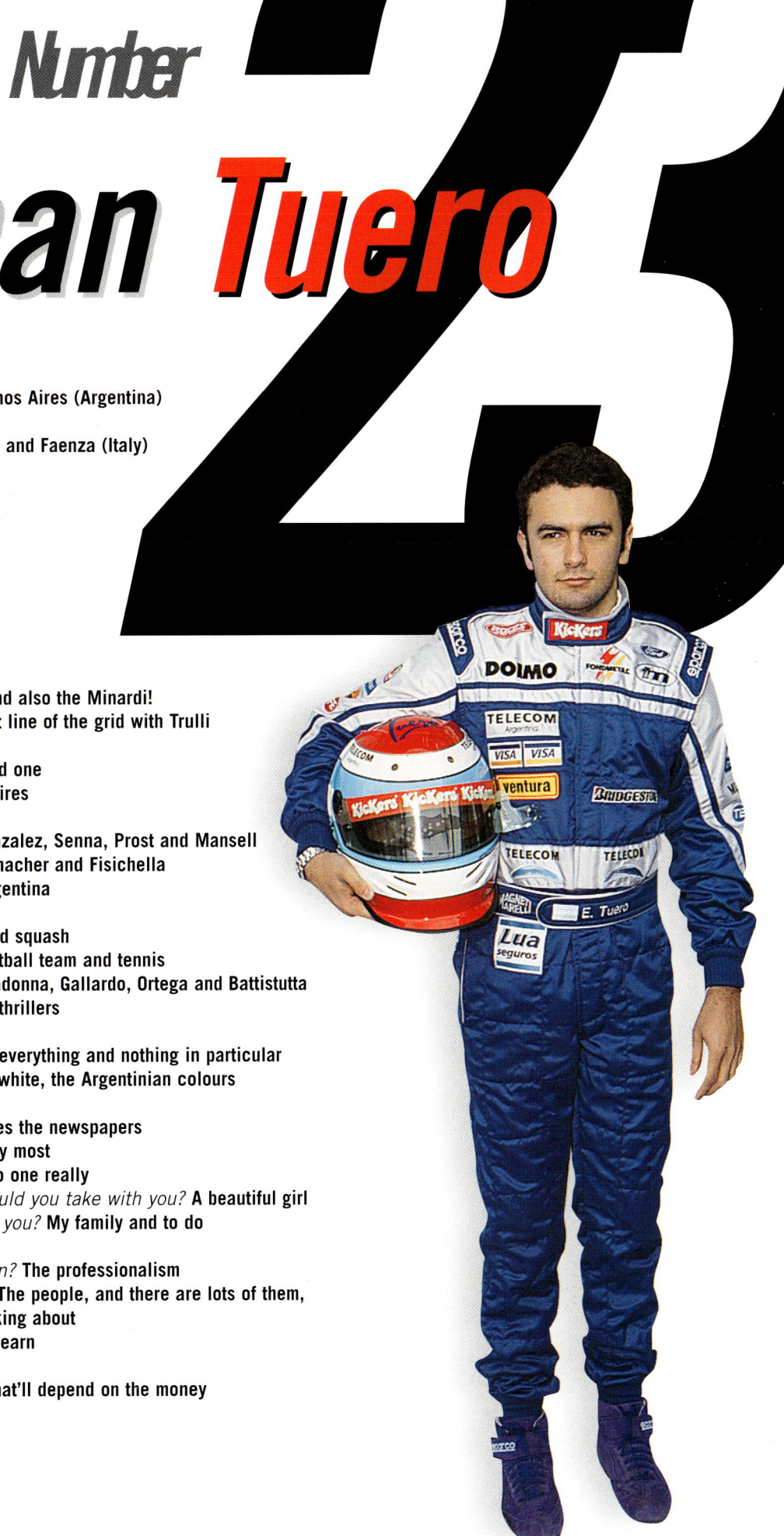

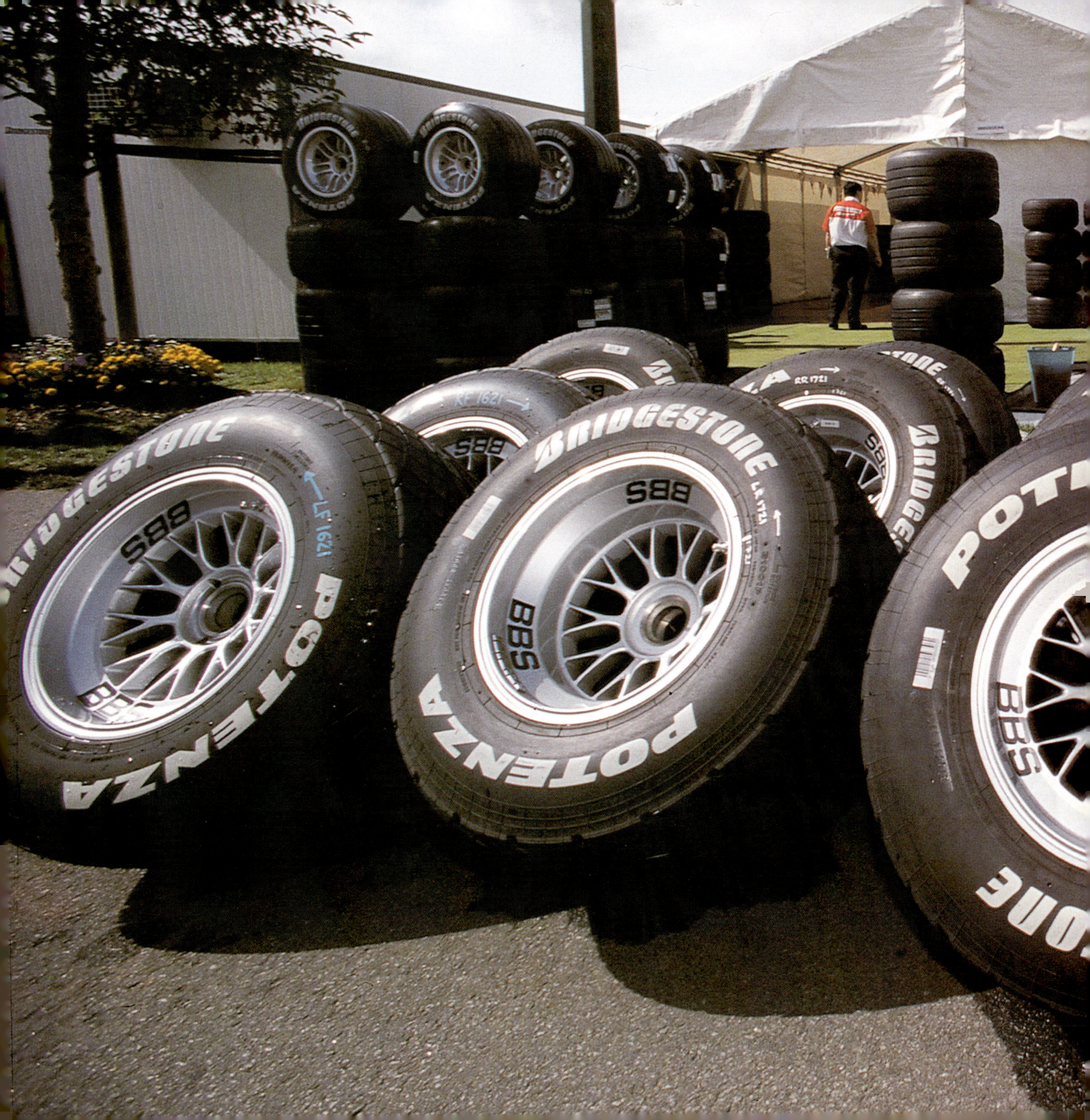
BRIDGESTONE
POTENZA
BBS
RR 1721

From the PADDOCK

Gerhard Berger
the last of the old school

When Gerhard Berger left Jerez in the evening of 26 October 1997, the last active F1 driver from the 1980s was walking away from the racing scene after a brilliant career.

In Vienna, ten days earlier, the Austrian had officially announced that he would retire after his 210th Grand Prix. Adored by women, this chivalrous playboy has always approached life at full speed. When team-mate Ayrton Senna was absorbed in endless hours of debriefing at McLaren, Gerhard shamelessly admitted he would prefer to go down to the beach to study pretty women rather than put the finishing touches to the fine-tuning of his racing car ...

His partnership with Senna was exceptional. He accepted the Brazilian's supremacy without rancour. When his friend died tragically in 1994, one day after compatriot Roland Ratzenberger had also perished, it made a huge impression on Gerhard. He hesitated for a time before driving again, then the lure of the track gripped him once more. Partnered by his friend Jean Alesi at Benetton, he was usually a top-six contender. In 1997, handicapped by serious sinus problems and then shattered by the death of his father in a plane crash, he returned from a brief exile with a stunning victory in Germany.

Despite his continuing self-belief, Gerhard has decided at the age of 38 that it is time to move on to other things. He is keen to spend time with his wife Ana and his three daughters, to divide his life between Monaco and Ibiza: skiing, sunshine and the sea, living away from the constraints of the racing track. The freshly retired Gerhard has already taken his place on the council of the Ayrton Senna Foundation and other tasks await him. The impending return to top-line racing of his former colleagues at BMW offers him a possible opportunity to keep a foot in the door as a technical adviser. And who knows? Once a winter has passed, perhaps the sirens of the motor racing world might coax him back into a car once again.

His victory for Ferrari at Monza on 11 September 1988, one month after the death of Enzo Ferrari, remains the highlight of his racing career. He is a walking anecdote machine and was a spectacular driver who never gave less than his best on the track. He had some horrifying accidents, and his escape from a fiery smash at Imola in 1989 elevated him to hero status.

Formula One needs these charismatic drivers, capable of any exploit, always ready to play a trick on their friends. From cream pies to throwing Senna's briefcase out of the door of a flying helicopter; from the moustache added to the Brazilian's passport photograph, to the surreptitious removal of Jean Alesi's mobile phone, subsequently used for calls all around the globe, Gerhard never missed a trick. In 1998, who will be able to provide his spark of good humour?

The great dreamer, the man for whom no exploit was too great, the knight of the impossible, the Don Juan of the pits - we miss you already.

Gerhard Berger
career statistics:

Born: 27 August 1959, Wörgl (Austria)
First GP: Austrian GP, 19 August 1984
Final GP: European GP (Jerez), 26 October 1997
Total GPs entered: 210
First point: Italian GP 1984 (his second race)
First podium: San Marino GP 1986
First win: Mexican GP 1986
Final win: German GP 1997
10 wins
17 seconds
21 thirds
12 pole positions
21 fastest laps
695 laps in the lead
385 points scored
Third in the world championship in 1988 and 1994
Fourth in 1990 and 91

Team history:
1984 : ATS BMW Turbo
1985 : Arrows BMW Turbo
1986 : Benetton BMW Turbo
1987-1988 : Ferrari Turbo
1989 : Ferrari
1990-1991-1992 : McLaren Honda
1993-1994-1995 : Ferrari
1996-1997 : Benetton Renault

ATOMIC
Shell

1
Mobil
UNITED COLORS OF BENETTON
FedEx
Mob

HONDA

BARCLAY
CAMOZZI
DeLonghi
17

Marlboro

MILD SEVEN
KOREAN AIR
KicKers
PI.SA
Agip

BENETTON

benetton

Marlboro
Agip

benetton
20

Glückssteile MOSER
ATOMIC SKI

Ken TYRRELL bows out...

On 20 February 1998, a simple press release from Tyrrell Racing announced that Ken Tyrrell and his son Bob were to leave the team which had carried their name for 30 years.

After selling his interest to American cigarette giant British American Tobacco last autumn, Ken was due to see out the 1998 season with his small team. The American company's plans for expansion are not due to take effect until next year. The 73-year-old wanted his career among motor sport's elite to end on a high. The last racing car of his era, the 026, looked to be well put together. It had a reasonable engine, two drivers who had plenty to prove and there seemed to be a reasonable chance he could bow out with a flourish.

And then, for reasons which are still clouded in mystery, the former timber merchant decided to call it a day. Did he go of his own accord or was he pushed? No-one is quite sure, but thus it was that one of the key characters in modern Formula One turned on his heels and left the sport via the back door.

Jackie Stewart, three times a world champion with Ken Tyrrell (in 1969-71-73), paid an eloquent tribute: 'His contribution to motor sport has been enormous,' he said. 'He has discovered and nurtured more young drivers than almost anyone else in the business. I am shocked to learn that Ken has decided to leave Formula One. Motor racing as a whole owes him a huge debt.'

Formula One has lost one of its key players, a man who was one of the very pillars of Grand Prix racing. Although it celebrated its 30th season in F1 last year, Tyrell's legendary team had been sliding inexorably towards the lower end of starting grids - and results sheets. Despite its four world titles (three for drivers, one for constructors) and its 33 race wins, Tyrrell failed to come to terms with the huge leap forward in investment which engulfed F1 at the beginning of the Eighties. And no money equalled no results. It was the start of a descent into relative obscurity. Tired of fighting simply to survive, Ken Tyrrell decided in 1997 to put an end to his suffering and to negotiate a deal while he could.

'Uncle Ken', as he was commonly known in F1, has always been a formidable talent-spotter. French stars François Cevert, Patrick Depailler, Didier Pironi and, more recently, Jean Alesi all earned their spurs with Tyrrell Racing. Going against contemporary F1 philosophy, Ken Tyrrell always preferred to take a driver for his ability rather than the size of his bank balance.

Time has simply flown by. After the golden age of Jackie Stewart and the fantastic experiment with the Tyrrell six-wheeler (the P34 raced by Scheckter, Depailler and Peterson in 1976-77), the marque scored its final victory at Detroit in 1983, courtesy of Michele Alboreto. There was a brief swansong in the early Nineties, mainly with Alesi ... and then there was a black hole. This famous team set up its base camp among the also-rans, in a shelter of anonymity.

Had the allure of motor racing finally flown? Was Uncle Ken finally resisting the siren call of Formula One? Will this recent retiree be able go from one day to the next without thinking about 30 thrilling years? In Barcelona, a few days before he announced his decision, he went to pay a visit to his staff. Was this a case of 'Until the next time', or was it a final farewell? The 1998 season will be long and the temptation to return will surely be too great. At least, that's what we all hope. We're already missing his big, toothy smile.

97

Grand Prix racing in the year 2000

From his office at 152A Walton Street, London, FIA president Max Mosley is working towards new ideas for Formula One from the year 2000. He is being helped in his aims by Bernie Ecclestone, one of his vice-presidents.

An ever-increasing number of applicants are canvassing for the right to stage a Grand Prix. In the Far East, China, Malaysia and Korea are all piling on the pressure to host an event as soon as possible, despite the current economic crisis in the region as a whole. Morocco, Lebanon and Cuba have all been high on the waiting-list, along with the United States, to which a return is an annual topic of speculation.

With the anti-tobacco advertising laws hovering like a cloud over Europe, the governing body has to keep a fanciful eye on other continents. The alternative proposed by some would not be easy to put into practice. It is already a strain for some circuits to recoup the substantial investments demanded by Formula One. It is hard to see them being deprived of a Grand Prix, even if they were to hold on to one on a one year in three system of rotation. The teams take a conservative view and do not want to see an increase in the number of races.

For Mosley, the ideal solution would be to put on 20 Grands Prix per annum. Working in tandem with F1's great power-broker Ecclestone, he would like to cut costs by reducing the race weekend to just two days, Saturday and Sunday. The loss of free practice on 20 Fridays would offset the cost of the extra three or four races. Formula One would save money and even get an extra seven days for possible holiday time. And TV rights would provide a significant rise in income which could be distributed to the teams. However, despite the possibility of extra revenue, nobody has yet been wooed by this proposal. The drivers have mixed opinions about a possible reduction in the duration of a race weekend.

Mosley, whose presidency runs until 2001, is keen to broaden Formula One's horizons. Grand Prix racing's TV ratings already rival the biggest box-office draws - the Olympic Games and soccer's World Cup - and a few more races would further strengthen the position of motor racing's number one attraction.

It is a question of time, diplomacy and patience between the teams and the federal authorities. How long will it be before Formula One cars are screaming through the streets of Marrakech, or Fidel Castro is handing the trophy to the winner of the Cuban Grand Prix? A long time ago, Juan Manuel Fangio was kidnapped on his way to Havana. Even in those far-off days, Formula One was an excellent lever for exerting pressure.

A Formula One Steering Wheel

Bernard Dudot, technical director of Prost GP, explains the functions on the steering wheel of Olivier Panis's Prost AP01

- Rev counter
- Engine speed
- Gear change
- Dashboard display
- Brake balance
- Differential
- Car-to-pits radio
- Down
- Up
- Clutch
- Rev counter
- Gear change
- Neutral
- Race start engine management
- Race start engine management
- Pit lane speed limiter
- Clutch

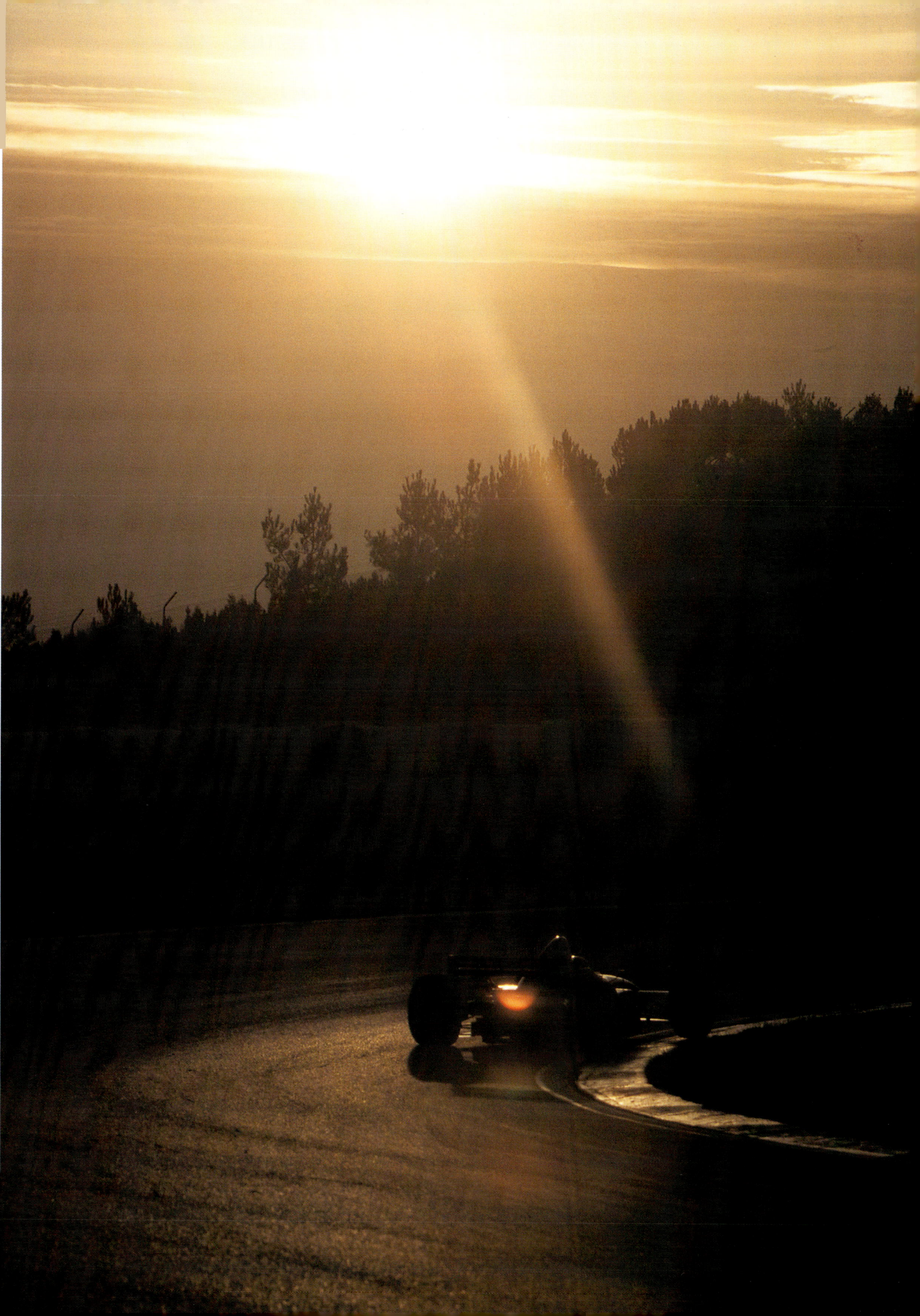

Postcards

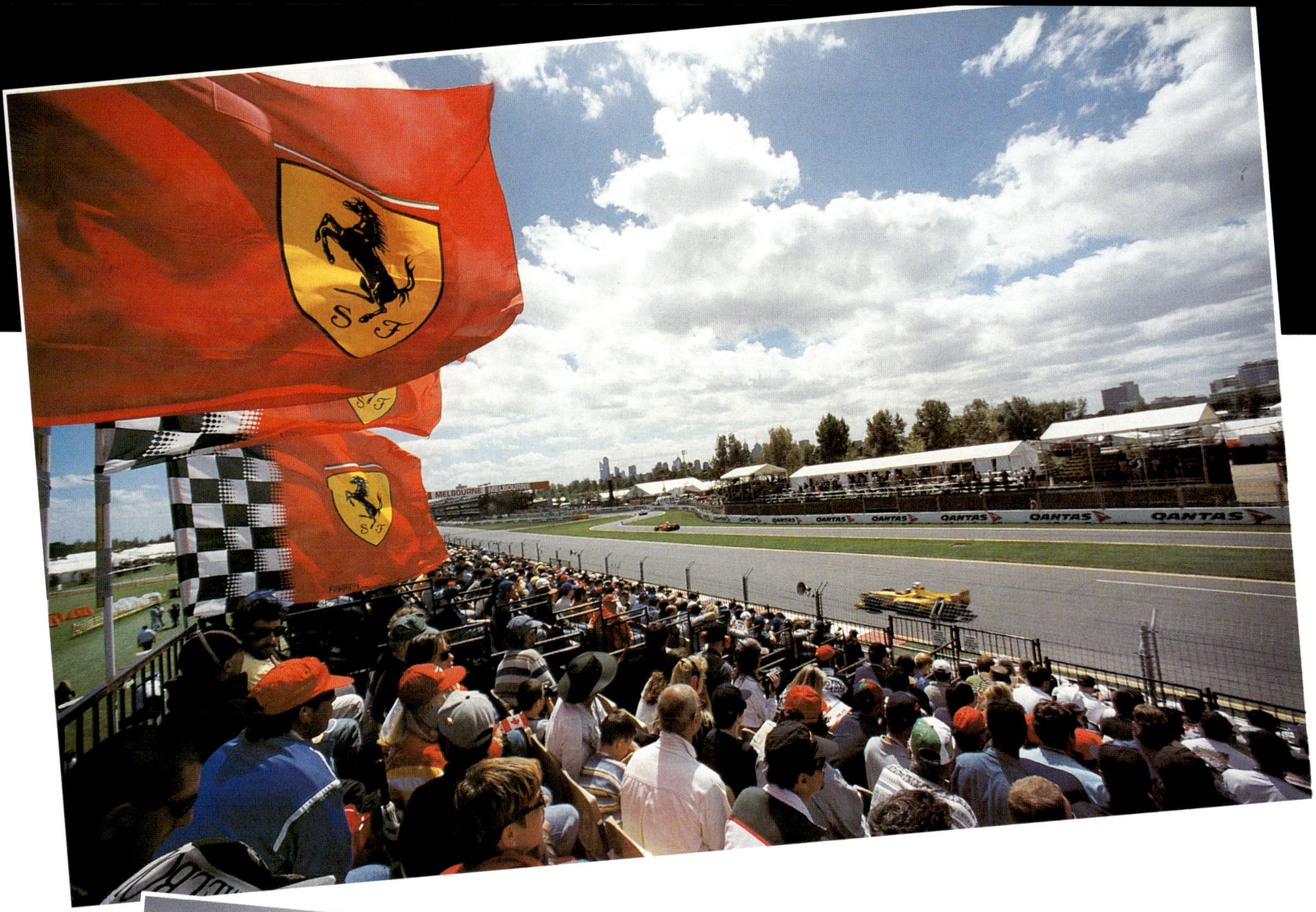

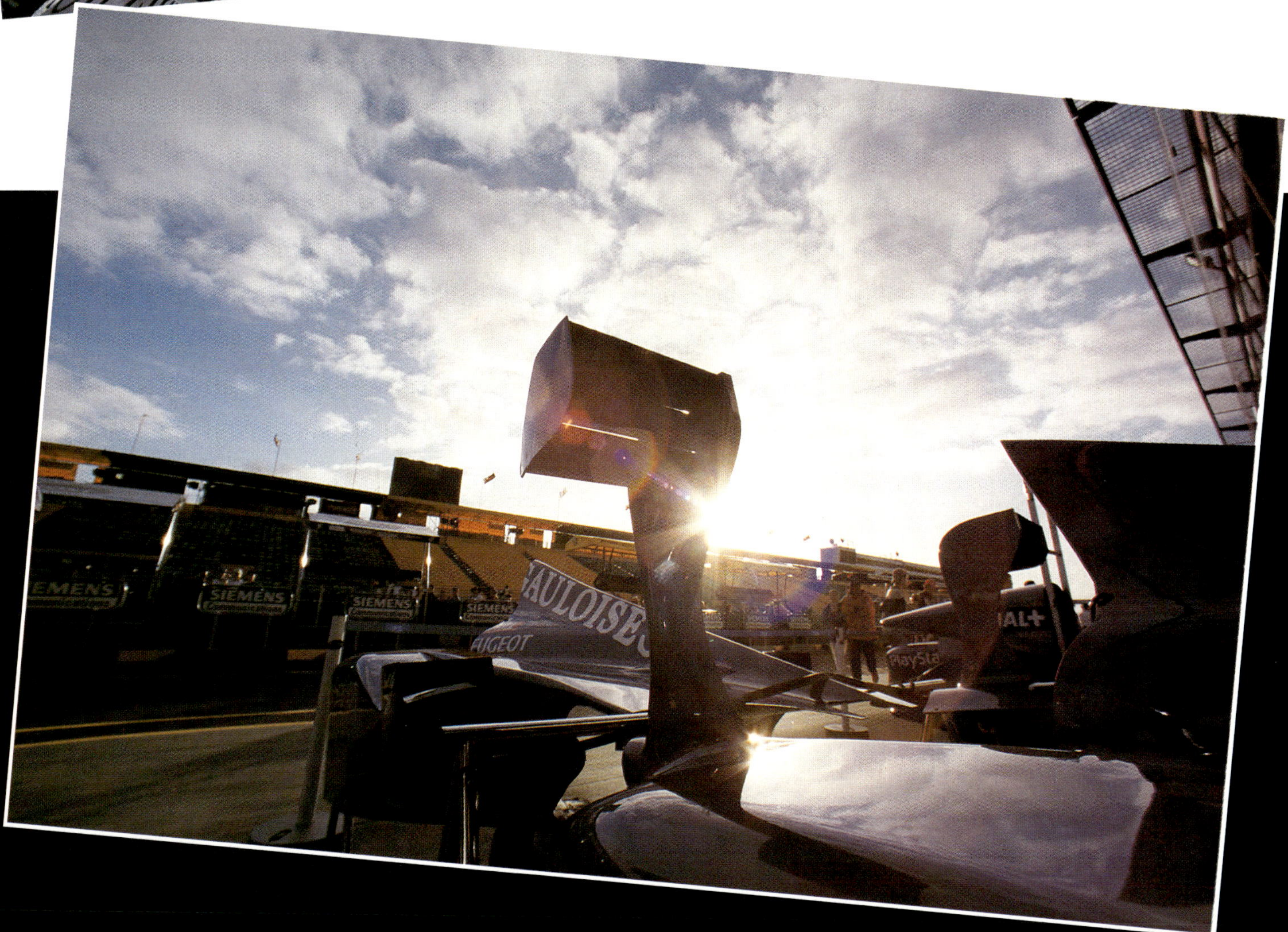

The Girls of Formula One

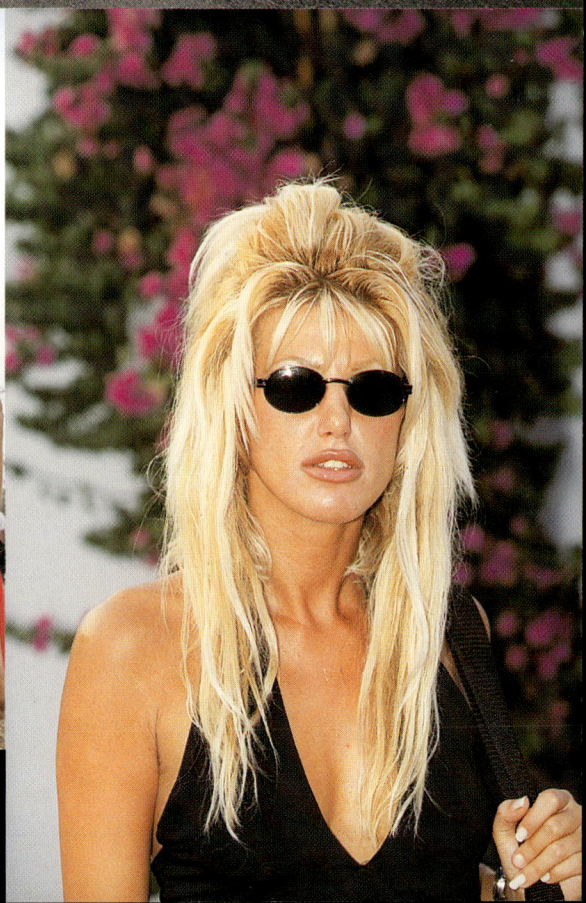

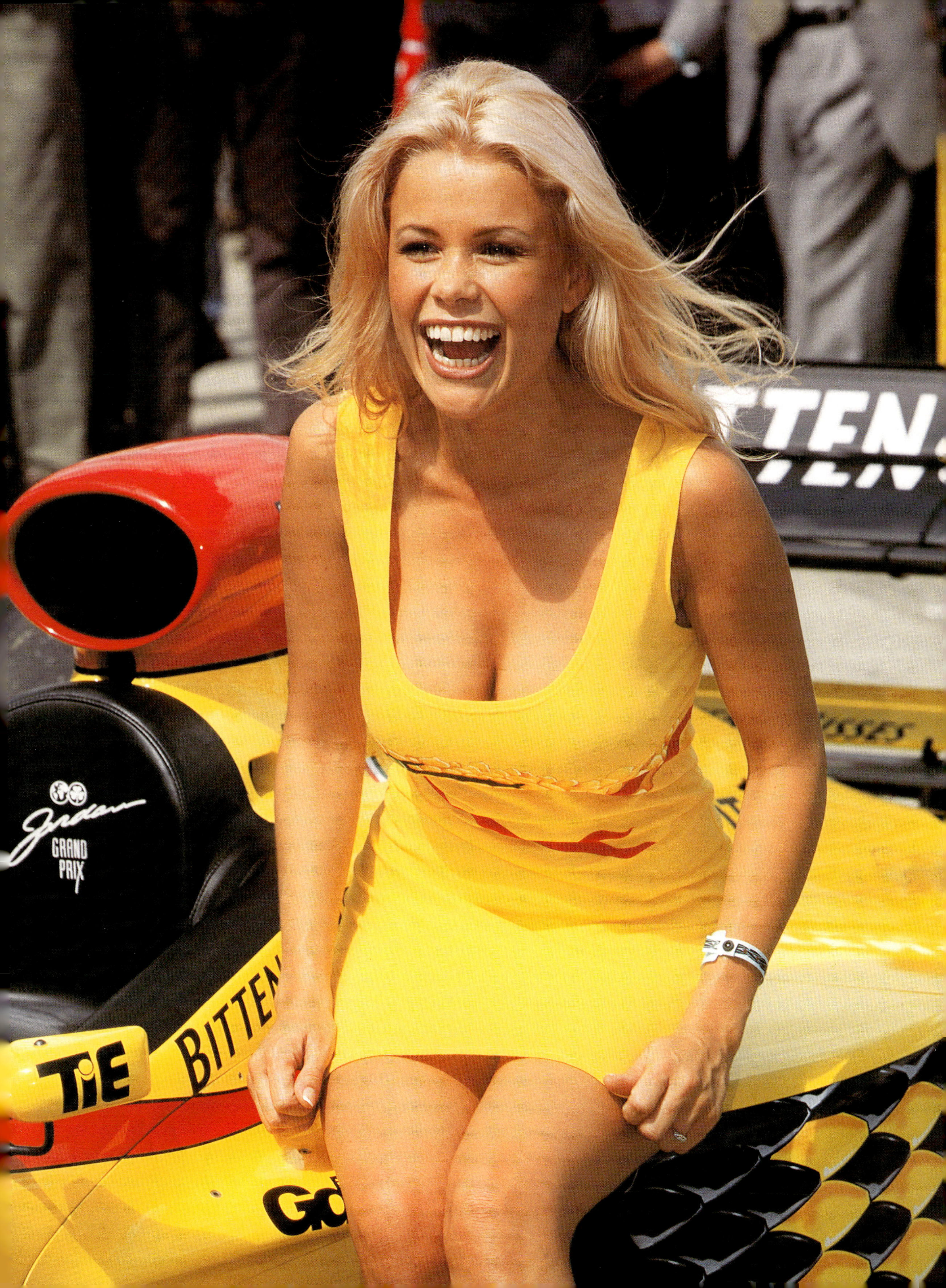
GRAND PRIX
TiE
BITTEN

Splashes of COLOUR

THE MAGIC OF INFRA RED

Like the teams in Formula One, photographers are always looking for something new. Infrared distorts the colours and gives a different view of Grand Prix action

West

MasterCard
HONDA
BENSON
MasterCard
BENSON & HEDGES
SHOWA SCANIA GOODYEAR DELPHI

Whatever happened to?

From 1990 until the eve of the 1997 Grand Prix of Europe at Jerez, no fewer than 91 drivers had taken part in a Formula One Grand Prix. Nowadays, a place in Formula One tends to be a bit like the ejector seat in a fighter plane. It takes colossal dedication just to get to F1 and it is harder still to hold on to your seat once you get there. There is only room for 20 or so drivers on the grid, so what on earth has happened to the rest of them?

Michael Andretti

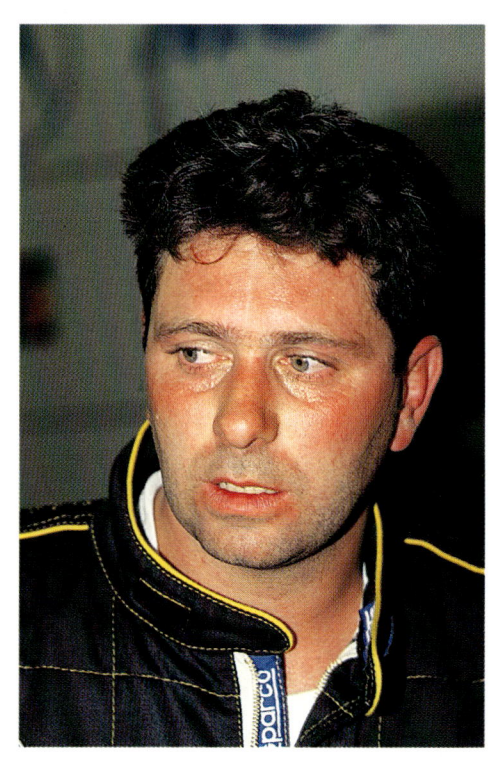

Eric Bernard

a

ADAMS Philippe (2)	Racing touring cars in his native Belgium
ALBORETO Michele (194)	Le Mans (Porsche)
ALESI Jean (135)	Formula 1 (Sauber)
ALLIOT Philippe (109)	Rally raids (Nissan) and Le Mans
ANDRETTI Michael (13)	IndyCar racing in the States (Newman-Haas)
APICELLA Marco (1)	Racing in Japan

b

BADOER Luca (35)	Ferrari F1 test driver
BAILEY Julian (7)	FIA GT Championship and Professional SportsCar (Lister)
BARBAZZA Fabrizio (8)	Retired from racing
BARILLA Paolo (15)	Working in the family business (Barilla pasta)
BARRICHELLO Rubens (81)	Formula 1 (Stewart GP)
BELMONDO Paul (7)	Porsche Supercup in France
BERETTA Olivier (10)	FIA GT Championship (Chrysler)
BERGER Gerhard (210)	Not racing at present
BERNARD Eric (45)	FIA GT Championship (Panoz)
BLUNDELL Mark (61)	IndyCar racing in the States (PacWest)
BOULLION Jean-Christophe (11)	Renault Spider Eurocup
BOUTSEN Thierry (163)	Sports car racing
BRABHAM David (24)	FIA GT Championship (Panoz)
BRUNDLE Martin (158)	TV commentator, Le Mans (Toyota)

Mark Blundell

c

CAFFI Alex (56)	Not racing at present
CAPELLI Ivan (93)	TV commentator
De CESARIS Andrea (208)	Not racing at present
CHIESA Andrea (3)	Working in the family business
COMAS Erik (59)	Le Mans (Nissan) and Indy 500 (Nissan)
COULTHARD David (58)	Formula 1 (McLaren)

d

DALMAS Yannick (24)	Professional SportsCar (Ferrari) and FIA GT Championship (Porsche)
DELETRAZ Jean-Denis (3)	FIA GT Championship
DINIZ Pedro (50)	Formula 1 (Arrows)
DONNELLY Martin (14)	Runs a Formula Three team in Britain

f

FISICHELLA Giancarlo (25)	Formula1 (Benetton)
FITTIPALDI Christian (40)	IndyCar racing in the States (Newman-Haas)
FOITEK Gregor (7)	Working in the family business
FONTANA Norberto	Not racing at present
FRENTZEN Heinz-Harald (65)	Formula 1 (Williams)

g

GACHOT Bertrand (47)	Touring car and GT racing in Japan
GIACOMELLI Bruno (69)	Racing in the Porsche Supercup
GOUNON Jean-Marc (9)	FIA GT Championship (Mercedes)
GROUILLARD Olivier (41)	Not racing at present
GUGELMIN Mauricio (74)	IndyCar racing in the States (PacWest)

h

HAKKINEN Mika (96)	Formula 1 (McLaren)
HERBERT Johnny (115)	Formula 1 (Sauber)
HILL Damon (84)	Formula 1 (Jordan)

ijk

INOUE Taki (18)	Not racing at present
IRVINE Eddie (65)	Formula 1 (Ferrari)
JOHANSSON Stefan (79)	Le Mans (Joest Porsche)
KATAYAMA Ukyo (95)	Le Mans (Toyota)

Martin Brundle

l

LAGORCE Franck (2)	Le Mans (Nissan)
LAMMERS Jan (23)	Le Mans (Nissan)
LAMY Pedro (32)	FIA GT Championship (Dodge)
LARINI Nicola (49)	Occasional test driver for Ferrari
LAVAGGI Giovanni (7)	Sports car racing
LEHTO J.J. (62)	IndyCar racing in the States (Hogan)

m

MANSELL Nigel (187)	Chamonix 24 Hours (Ford), possibly some British Touring Car Championship races and also runs a golf centre
MAGNUSSEN Jan (18)	Formula 1 (Stewart GP)
MARQUES Tarso (11)	Not racing at present
MARTINI Pier-Luigi (119)	Le Mans (BMW)
MODENA Stefano (70)	Touring car racing
MONTERMINI Andrea (21)	Le Mans (Nissan)
MORBIDELLI Gianni (67)	British Touring Car Championship (Volvo) and Le Mans (Nissan)
MORENO Roberto (42)	Looking for drives in America

n

NAKAJIMA Satoru (74)	Runs Nakajima Planning, with teams in F3 and Formula Nippon in Japan
NAKANO Shinji (17)	Formula 1 (Minardi)
NANNINI Alessandro (77)	FIA GT Championship
NASPETTI Emanuele (6)	Italian Touring Car Championship
NODA Hideki (3)	Formula Indy Lights

p

PANIS Olivier (59)	Formula 1 (Prost GP)
PAPIS Massimiliano (7)	IndyCar racing in the States (Arciero-Wells)
PATRESE Riccardo (256)	Not racing at present
PIQUET Nelson (204)	Working in business and Le Mans (McLaren BMW)
PIRRO Emanuele (37)	German Touring Car Championship (Audi)
PROST Alain (199)	F1 team owner

r-s

RATZENBERGER Roland (1)	Killed during practice for the 1994 San Marino GP
ROSSET Ricardo (16)	Formula 1 (Tyrrell)
SALO Mika (52)	Formula 1 (Arrows)
SCHIATTARELLA Domenico (6)	Not racing at present
SCHNEIDER Bernd (9)	FIA GT Championship (Mercedes)
SCHUMACHER Michael (102)	Formula 1 (Ferrari)
SCHUMACHER Ralf (17)	Formula 1 (Jordan)
SENNA Ayrton (161)	Killed during 1994 San Marino GP
SUZUKI Aguri (64)	Le Mans (Nissan)
SUZUKI Toshio (2)	GT racing in Japan

Nelson Piquet

t-v

TARQUINI Gabriele (38)	German Touring Car Championship (Honda)
TRULLI Jarno (13)	Formula 1 (Prost GP)
VAN DE POELE Eric (5)	Professional SportsCar (Ferrari)
VERSTAPPEN Jos (48)	Not racing at present
VILLENEUVE Jacques (32)	Formula 1 (Williams)

w

WARWICK Derek (147)	British Touring Car Championship (Vauxhall)
WENDLINGER Karl (41)	FIA GT Championship (Dodge)
WURZ Alexander (3)	Formula 1 (Benetton)

z

ZANARDI Alessandro (25)	IndyCar racing in the States (Ganassi)

Nigel Mansell

NB : The figure in brackets indicates the number of Grands Prix contested. Only those drivers who have started for at least one race have been included. No account has been taken of those who have entered but who failed to qualify.

Riccardo Patrese

Jacques Villeneuve and Alessandro Zanardi

Grands Prix

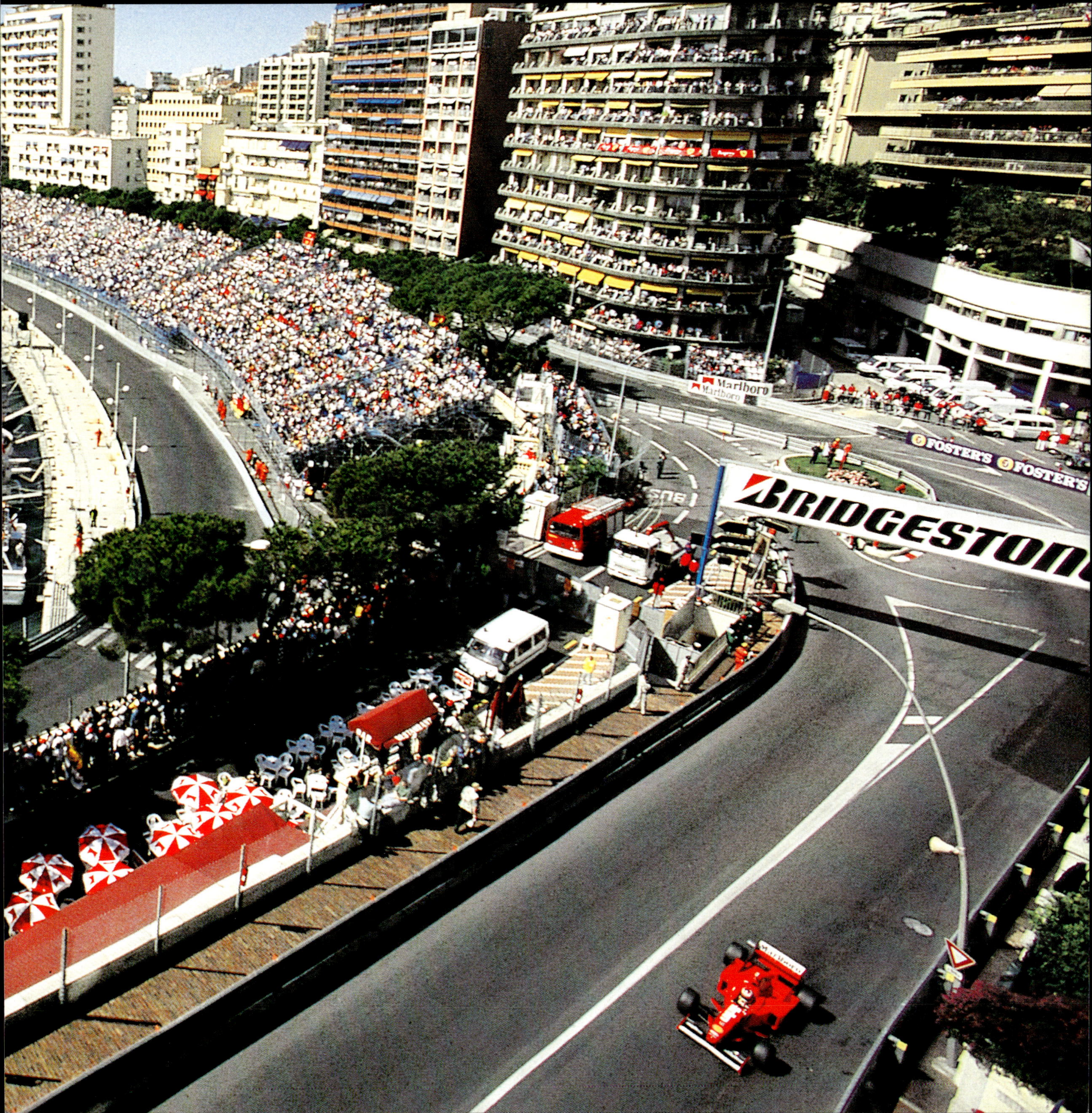
BRIDGESTONE
FOSTER'S
FOSTER'S
Marlboro

Australian Grand Prix
Melbourne

Sunday 8 March 1998

ADDRESS: Albert Park
Grand Prix Circuit,
Melbourne, Victoria 3205
AUSTRALIA

Tel:
00 61 3 92 58 71 00
Fax:
00 61 3 96 99 37 27

After a decade in the southern city of Adelaide, the Australian Grand Prix has been switched to Melbourne for a variety of reasons, both political and financial. The Formula One fraternity are made welcome in Albert Park, on the outskirts of the city centre. The organisation is absolutely first-class and it is a sumptuous setting for the opening race of the year. The track winds its way around a lake populated by black-and-white swans. You can understand why some ecologists were so against the establishment of the event. It is the beginning of autumn when the race takes place and the sun is still powerful. The beach is only a few hundred metres from the circuit but, unfortunately, the start of a new term does not allow time for dawdling around in the Australian sunshine.

START TIME: 14.00 (03.00 in Britain), 58 laps of a 5.302 km circuit, a total distance of 307.52 km

CROWD FIGURES IN 1997: 154,000 spectators over 3 days

DAVID COULTHARD'S VIEW OF *MELBOURNE*:

'Naturally I have fond memories of this circuit because I won here last year. The Australians know how to put on a good welcome and the first race of the year has a great atmosphere. The track lacks a little bit of grip, because it's not a permanent facility, but the corners link together nicely. Even though there aren't any really quick corners, it's easy to build up a good rhythm.'

Australian Grand Prix 1997

Starting grid:
1 J. Villeneuve	Williams Renault	1'29"369
2 H-H. Frentzen	Williams Renault	1'31"123
3 M. Schumacher	Ferrari	1'31"472
4 D. Coulthard	McLaren Mercedes	1'31"531
5 E. Irvine	Ferrari	1'31"881
6 M. Hakkinen	McLaren Mercedes	1'31"971

etc.

Race result:
1	D. Coulthard	McLaren Mercedes	in 1h 30'28"718
2	M. Schumacher	Ferrari	+20"046
3	M. Hakkinen	McLaren Mercedes	+22" 177
4	G. Berger	Benetton Renault	+22"841
5	O. Panis	Prost Mugen Honda	+1'00"308
6	N. Larini	Sauber Petronas	+1'36"040
7	S. Nakano	Prost Mugen Honda	+2 laps
8	H-H. Frentzen	Williams Renault	+2 laps
9	J. Trulli	Minardi Hart	+3 laps
10	P. Diniz	Arrows Yamaha	+4 laps

Fastest lap: H-H. Frentzen (Williams Renault) in 1'30"585

AUSTRALIAN GP Winners

1997 : D. COULTHARD (McLaren)
1996 : D. HILL (Williams)
1995 : D. HILL (Williams)
1994 : N. MANSELL (Williams)

1993 : A. SENNA (McLaren)
1992 : R. PATRESE (Williams)
1991 : A. SENNA (McLaren)
1990 : N. PIQUET (Benetton) etc.

Alain PROST (1986-88), Ayrton SENNA (1991-93) and Damon HILL (1995-96) have all won the Australian GP twice.

The first-ever winner was Keke Rosberg (Williams) in 1985.

Grande Premio do Brasil

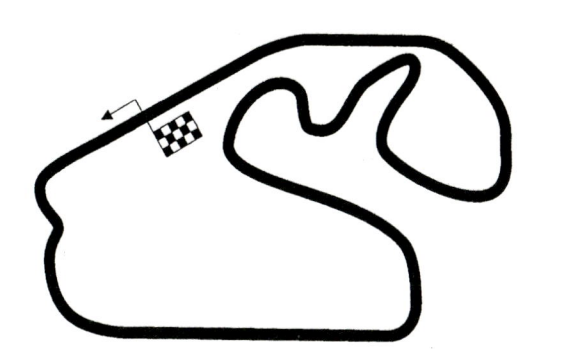

Brazilian Grand Prix
Interlagos

Sunday 29 March 1998

ADDRESS: AUTODROMO
DE INTERLAGOS
Av. Senador Teotonio Vilela 261
SAO PAOLO, BRAZIL

Tel:
00 55 21 521 99 11
Fax:
00 55 21 242 44 94

The circuit lies 16 kilometres from the centre of São Paolo, in the suburb of Interlagos. Rubens Barrichello, current leader of the Brazilian F1 contingent, was born only a few hundred metres from the track. It is amid an enormous metropolis which never ceases to grow, With the year 2000 fast approaching, the population borders on 20 million inhabitants - the biggest city in the world. Ever-increasing poverty and sordid favelas sit uneasily next to the luxury modern skyscrapers and hotels where the F1 folk stay.

The Grand Prix's former home in Rio has turned to staging IndyCar races, where a number of Brazilian drivers are making a name for themselves. In Brazil Formula One is at something of a low ebb at the moment. The Interlagos circuit has its attractions but the whole world of F1 thinks back with fond memories to Rio ...

START TIME: 13.00 (17.00 in Britain), 71 laps of a 4.325 km circuit, a total distance of 307.075 km

CROWD FIGURES IN 1997: 55,000 spectators

DAVID COULTHARD'S VIEW OF *INTERLAGOS*:

'It is a very demanding track which runs anti-clockwise, unlike all the others. It is a hard race physically, because of the heat. But I like the mixture of slow and fast corners and the level of grip is not too bad.
The Brazilian fans are brilliant - what an atmosphere!'

Brazilian Grand Prix 1997

Starting grid:
1	J. Villeneuve	Williams Renault	1'16"004
2	M. Schumacher	Ferrari	1'16"594
3	G. Berger	Benetton Renault	1'16"644
4	M. Hakkinen	McLaren Mercedes	1'16"694
5	O. Panis	Prost Mugen Honda	1'16"756
6	J. Alesi	Benetton Renault	1'16"757

etc.

Fastest lap: J. Villeneuve (Williams Renault) in 1'18"397

Race result:
1	J. Villeneuve	Williams Renault	in 1h 36'06"990
2	G. Berger	Benetton Renault	+4"190
3	O. Panis	Prost Mugen Honda	+15"870
4	M. Hakkinen	McLaren Honda	+33"033
5	M. Schumacher	Ferrari	+33"731
6	J. Alesi	Benetton Renault	+34"020
7	J. Herbert	Sauber Petronas	+50"912
8	G. Fisichella	Jordan Peugeot	+1'00"639
9	H-H. Frentzen	Williams Renault	+1'15"402
10	D. Coulthard	McLaren Mercedes	+1 lap
11	N. Larini	Sauber Petronas	+1 lap
12	J. Trulli	Minardi Hart	+1 lap
13	M. Salo	Tyrrell Ford	+1 lap
14	S. Nakano	Prost Mugen Honda	+1 lap
15	J. Verstappen	Tyrrell Ford	+2 laps
16	E. Irvine	Ferrari	+2 laps
17	D. Hill	Arrows Yamaha	+3 laps
18	U. Katayama	Minardi Hart	+5 laps

BRAZILIAN GP Winners

1997 : J. VILLENEUVE (Williams)
1996 : D. HILL (Williams)
1995 : M. SCHUMACHER (Benetton)
1994 : M. SCHUMACHER (Benetton)

1993 : A. SENNA (McLaren)
1992 : N. MANSELL (Williams)
1991 : A. SENNA (McLaren)
1990 : A. PROST (McLaren) etc.

Alain PROST has won in Brazil a record six times (1982-84-85-87-88-90).
Emerson FITTIPALDI won the first-ever Brazilian GP, at Interlagos in 1973.

Gran Premio de Argentina

Argentinian Grand Prix
Buenos Aires

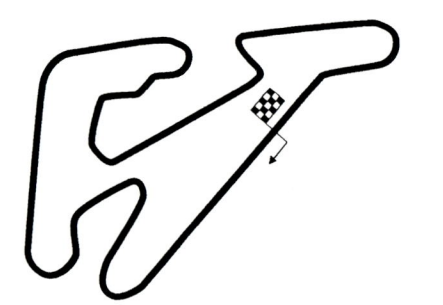

Sunday 12 April 1998

ADDRESS: Circuito Almirante-Brown
Automovil Club Argentina
Avenida del Libertador 1850
1461 BUENOS AIRES, ARGENTINA

Tel:
00 54 18 01 18 37
Fax:
00 54 18 01 39 72

The circuit lies 15 kilometres to the south of Buenos Aires. After being dropped from the F1 calendar in 1982, the race was reinstated in 1995. The old South American double-header was back. The late Juan Manuel Fangio and, subsequently, Carlos Reutemann did much of the donkey work to enable it to happen. The track has been much modified to meet the FIA's draconian demands and today it meets every required standard. The years may have passed by, but the Argentinians have lost none of their fervour or their enthusiasm.
The idol of the crowd will be local boy Esteban Tuero, making his F1 début before he has even reached the age of 20. The Grand Prix tickets bear his image and hundreds of posters have already been printed in his honour.
It really will be carnival time in grandstands which were already quite lively enough to start with.

START TIME: 13.00 (17.00 in Britain), 72 laps of a 4.259 km circuit, a total distance of 306.648 km

CROWD FIGURES IN 1997: 70,000 spectators

DAVID COULTHARD'S VIEW OF *BUENOS AIRES*:
'I know that Jacques Villeneuve calls this a real Mickey Mouse circuit. It's true that the track is narrow and twisty and there is not a great deal of grip. It's disappointing that there isn't one really fast, challenging corner. But Argentina is a beautiful country. The crowds are really enthusiastic and they are an impressive sight.'

Argentinian Grand Prix 1997

Starting grid:

1	J. Villeneuve	Williams Renault	1'24"473
2	H-H. Frentzen	Williams Renault	1'25"271
3	O. Panis	Prost Mugen Honda	1'25"491
4	M. Schumacher	Ferrari	1'25"773
5	R. Barrichello	Stewart Ford	1'25"942
6	R. Schumacher	Jordan Peugeot	1'26"218

etc.

Fastest lap: G. Berger (Benetton Renault) in 1'27"981

Race result:

1	J. Villeneuve	Williams Renault	in 1h52'01"715
2	E. Irvine	Ferrari	+0"979
3	R. Schumacher	Jordan Peugeot	+12"089
4	J. Herbert	Sauber Petronas	+29"919
5	M. Hakkinen	McLaren Mercedes	+30"351
6	G. Berger	Benetton Renault	+31"393
7	J. Alesi	Benetton Renault	+46"359
8	M. Salo	Tyrrell Ford	+1 lap
9	J. Trulli	Minardi Hart	+1 lap
10	J. Magnussen	Stewart Ford	+2 laps

ARGENTINIAN GP Winners

1997 : J. VILLENEUVE (Williams)
1996 : D. HILL (Williams)
1995 : D. HILL (Williams)
1981 : N. PIQUET (Brabham)

1980 : A. JONES (Williams)
1979 : J. LAFFITE (Ligier)
1978 : M. ANDRETTI (Lotus)
1977 : J. SCHECKTER (Wolf) etc.

Alberto ASCARI (Ferrari) won the very first Argentine GP, on 18 January 1953 in Buenos Aires.

San Marino Grand Prix
Imola

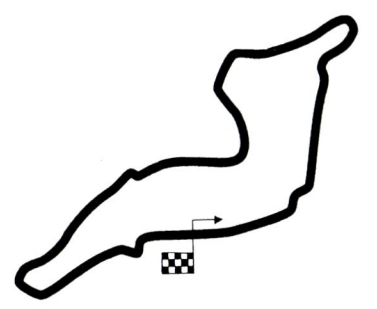

Gran Premio di San Marino

Sunday 25 April 1998

ADDRESS: Autodromo Enzo et Dino Ferrari
SAGIS SPA Viale Dante
40026 IMOLA (Bo) ITALY

Tel: 00 39 542 31 444
Fax: 00 39 542 30 420

Lying 35 kilometres to the south-east of Bologna, Imola traditionally marks the beginning of the Formula One season in Europe after the long-distance haul to Australia and South America. And the return to Europe means that teams can relax once more in their increasingly luxurious motorhomes.
The surrounding countryside has more than an air of Tuscany. It is springtime, the famous pasta is as good as always and the Italian reception is ever warm. The high-spirited tifosi make this first European race of the season an occasion to savour.

START TIME : 13.00 in Britain, 63 laps of a 4.892 km circuit, a total distance of 308.196 km.

CROWD FIGURES IN 1997: 90,000 spectators

DAVID COULTHARD'S VIEW OF *IMOLA*:

'I like Imola. The chicanes have been well designed and are reasonably quick. It's a track which puts an emphasis on strong power and good brakes. Tamburello is a particularly good corner, and still very quick. The tifosi give Ferrari an absolutely fantastic reception but the McLaren Mercedes team seems quite popular too.'

San Marino Grand Prix 1997

Starting grid:

1	J. Villeneuve	Williams Renault	1'23"303
2	H-H. Frentzen	Williams Renault	1'23"646
3	M. Schumacher	Ferrari	1'23"955
4	O. Panis	Prost Mugen Honda	1'24"075
5	R. Schumacher	Jordan Peugeot	1'24"075
6	G. Fisichella	Jordan Peugeot	1'24"596

etc.

Race result:

1	H-H. Frentzen	Williams Renault	in 1h 31'00"673
2	M. Schumacher	Ferrari	+1"237
3	E. Irvine	Ferrari	+1'18"343
4	G. Fisichella	Jordan Peugeot	+1'23"388
5	J. Alesi	Benetton Renault	+1 lap
6	M. Hakkinen	McLaren Mercedes	+1 lap
7	N. Larini	Sauber Petronas	+1 lap
8	O. Panis	Prost Mugen Honda	+1 lap
9	M. Salo	Tyrrell Ford	+2 laps
10	J. Verstappen	Tyrrell Ford	+2 laps
11	U. Katayama	Minardi Hart	+3 laps

Fastest lap: H-H. Frentzen (Williams Renault) in 1'25"531

SAN MARINO GP Winners

1997 : H.H. FRENTZEN (Williams)
1996 : D. HILL (Williams)
1995 : D. HILL (Williams)
1994 : M. SCHUMACHER (Benetton)
1993 : A. PROST (Williams)
1992 : N. MANSELL (Williams)
1991 : A. SENNA (McLaren)
1990 : R. PATRESE (Williams) etc.

Ayrton SENNA (1988-89-91) and Alain PROST (1984-86-93) have each won the race three times.
Nelson Piquet won the first San Marino GP on 3 May 1981; Piquet also won Imola's first-ever world championship race, the Italian GP of 1980

Grand Prix de Monaco

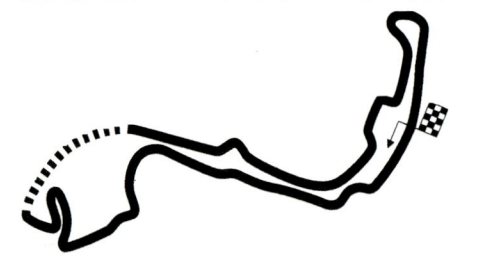

Monaco Grand Prix
Monte-Carlo

SUNDAY 24 MAY 1998

ADDRESS: AUTOMOBILE CLUB
DE MONACO
23 Bd Albert 1er
98012 MONACO Cedex

Tel:
00 377 93 15 26 00
Fax:
00 377 93 25 80 08

The circuit runs around the principality of Monaco, 18 kilometres to the east of Nice. No question, this is the most prestigious F1 race of them all and is the most famous the world over. Its reputation is never likely to be surpassed. No other round of the world championship offers such diverse charms and the spectacle of seeing F1 cars racing round the streets is gripping in itself. The sound of the engines in full cry is astounding.

The organisation is faultless, you can spot a few curious stars from the Cannes film festival, some of the world's most beautiful women, the ocean-blue expanse beyond the circuit, the legendary corners ... in short, everything about Monaco is magical.

There are those who knock it because it is ill-suited to modern F1 cars, because of its upper-class air and draconian police force, but don't miss a chance to drag yourself along to the fringe of the Mediterranean during Ascension weekend. Life is expensive on the Côte d'Azur, but you won't regret a moment.

START TIME: 13.30 in Britain, 78 laps of a 3.328 km circuit, a total distance of 259.584 km.

CROWD FIGURES IN 1997: 105,000 spectators

DAVID COULTHARD'S VIEW OF *MONACO*:

'Every year I tell myself the same thing, that it's mad to have a Grand Prix here. The circuit puts you under more mental strain than it does physical. You always wonder how on earth you can get a good lap on such a track. It's fantastically rewarding when you do get it right. There is a fascination with driving past these guard-rails which are absolutely everywhere. It is a unique event and it is one heck of a challenge.'

Monaco Grand Prix 1997

Starting grid:

1	H-H. Frentzen	Williams Renault	1'18"216
2	M. Schumacher	Ferrari	1'18"235
3	J. Villeneuve	Williams Renault	1'18"583
4	G. Fisichella	Jordan Peugeot	1'18"665
5	D. Coulthard	McLaren Mercedes	1'18"779
6	R. Schumacher	Jordan Peugeot	1'18"943

etc.

> Fastest lap: M. Schumacher (Ferrari) in 1'53"315

Race result:

1	M. Schumacher	Ferrari	in 2h00'05"654
2	R. Barrichello	Stewart Ford	+53"306
3	E. Irvine	Ferrari	+1'22"108
4	O. Panis	Prost Mugen Honda	+1'44"402
5	M. Salo	Tyrrell Ford	+1 lap
6	G. Fisichella	Jordan Peugeot	+1 lap
7	J. Magnussen	Stewart Ford	+1 lap
8	J. Verstappen	Tyrrell Ford	+2 laps
9	G. Berger	Benetton Renault	+2 laps
10	U. Katayama	Minardi Hart	+2 laps

MONACO GP Winners:

1997 : M. SCHUMACHER (Ferrari)
1996 : O. PANIS (Ligier)
1995 : M. SCHUMACHER (Benetton)
1994 : M. SCHUMACHER (Benetton)
1993 : A. SENNA (McLaren)
1992 : A. SENNA (McLaren)

1991 : A. SENNA (McLaren)
1990 : A. SENNA (McLaren) etc.

Ayrton SENNA is the most successful driver in the history of Monaco, with six victories (1987-89-90-91-92-93).

Graham HILL triumphed five times (1963-64-65-68-69).
Alain PROST scored four wins (1984-85-86-88).
Juan Manuel FANGIO (Alfa Romeo) won the first world championship race in Monaco, on 21 May 1950.

Gran Premio de España

Spanish Grand Prix
Barcelona

SUNDAY 10 MAY 1998

ADDRESS : Circuit de Cataluna
Carretera de Granollers, km 2
O8160 MONTMELO (BA)
SPAIN

Tel:
00 34 3 57 19 700
Fax:
00 34 3 57 23 061

Twenty kilometres north of Barcelona, the circuit was built at the same time as the huge stadia which hosted the 1992 Olympic Games. An ultra-modern facility, it meets all the standards demanded by contemporary Formula One. There are huge grandstands, sizeable run-off areas in all the danger zones and the undulating circuit offers spectators a great view - as well as easy access. It is in the same mould as Magny-Cours, with excellent safety facilities. Drivers appreciate the technical nature of the track and the high-speed corners.
Unfortunately, the one thing it lacks is character. The Catalans don't exactly stampede to get in and it has the lowest attendance figures of the season.

START TIME: 13.00 in Britain, 65 laps of a 4.727 km circuit, a total distance of 307.114 km.

CROWD FIGURES IN 1997 : 45,000 spectators

DAVID COULTHARD'S VIEW OF
BARCELONA:
'It is a fairly demanding track and one of the most wearing on the car. Tyres don't last long, either. There is no shortage of quick corners, which is something of a rarity in modern F1. There is plenty of grip, too, although the bad news is that it is a very difficult circuit on which to overtake.'

Spanish Grand Prix 1997

Starting grid:

1	J. Villeneuve	Williams Renault	1'16"525
2	H-H. Frentzen	Williams Renault	1'16"791
3	D. Coulthard	McLaren Mercedes	1'17"521
4	J. Alesi	Benetton Renault	1'17"717
5	M. Hakkinen	McLaren Mercedes	1'17"737
6	G. Berger	Benetton Renault	1'18"O41

etc.

Fastest lap: G. Fisichella (Jordan Peugeot) in 1'22"242

Race result:

1	J. Villeneuve	Williams Renault	in 1h30'35"896
2	O. Panis	Prost Mugen Honda	+5"804
3	J. Alesi	Benetton Renault	+12"534
4	M. Schumacher	Ferrari	+17"979
5	J. Herbert	Sauber Petronas	+27"986
6	D. Coulthard	McLaren Mercedes	+29"744
7	M. Hakkinen	McLaren Mercedes	+48"785
8	H-H. Frentzen	Williams Renault	+1'04"139
9	G. Fisichella	Jordan Peugeot	+1'04"767
10	G. Berger	Benetton Renault	+1'05"670
11	J. Verstappen	Tyrrell Ford	+1 lap
12	E. Irvine	Ferrari	+1 lap
13	J. Magnussen	Stewart Ford	+1 lap
14	G. Morbidelli	Sauber Petronas	+2 laps
15	J. Trulli	Minardi Hart	+2 laps

SPANISH GP Winners

1997 : J. VILLENEUVE (Williams)
1996 : M. SCHUMACHER (Ferrari)
1995 : M. SCHUMACHER (Benetton)
1994 : D. HILL (Williams)

1993 : A. PROST (Williams)
1992 : N. MANSELL (Williams)
1991 : N. MANSELL (Williams)
1990 : A. PROST (Ferrari) (at Jerez) etc.

Alain PROST (1988-90-93) and Jackie STEWART (1969-70-73) have both claimed three victories in the Spanish GP. Juan Manuel FANGIO (Alfa Romeo) was the first-ever Spanish GP winner. The race took place on the street circuit of Pedralbes, close to Barcelona, on 28 October 1951.

Grand Prix du Canada

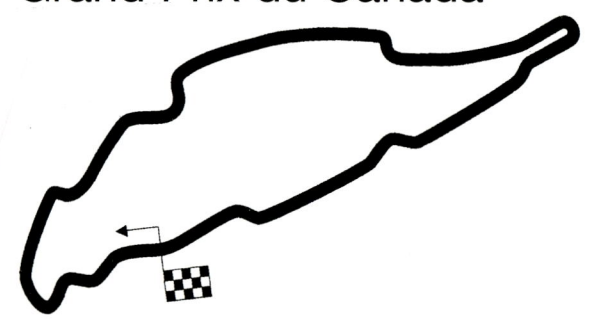

Canadian Grand Prix
Montréal

SUNDAY 7 JUNE 1998

ADDRESS: Circuit Gilles Villeneuve
Bassin Olympique, Ile Notre Dame
MONTREAL, QUEBEC H3C 1AO
CANADA

Tel:
00 1 514 39 24 731
Fax:
00 1 514 39 20 007

The track can be found only a few kilometres from the city centre, on the Ile Notre Dame - home of the 1967 International Exhibition and selected events at the 1976 Olympic Games. Racegoers tend not to bother bringing their cars along, but rely on public transport.
The participation of the reigning world champion will cause quite a stir in Quebec. The street walls in Montreal are adorned with countless posters paying tribute to the national hero. Jacques has promised that he will do everything he can to add his name to list of winners at the circuit which already bears the name of his late father. Just six hours by air from mainland Europe, the combination of Quebec's warm welcome, North American charm and a traditionally exciting race make Montreal one of the most popular races of the season. Disturbed by this tidal-wave invasion, only the marmots on the island appear less than fully enthusiastic about F1.

START TIME: 13.00 (18.00 in Britain), 69 laps of a 4.421 km circuit, a total distance of 305.049 km.

CROWD FIGURES IN 1997: 102,829 spectators

DAVID COULTHARD'S VIEW OF *MONTREAL* :

'In some ways this track is a bit like Monza and Imola, with long straights and slow corners. The only really quick corner is the one where Olivier Panis had his accident last year. The track is not very grippy because it is only used once a year. The atmosphere in Montreal is always really good and the local people are wonderful.'

Canadian Grand Prix 1997

Starting grid:

1	M. Schumacher	Ferrari	1'18"095
2	J. Villeneuve	Williams Renault	1'18"108
3	R. Barrichello	Stewart Ford	1'18"388
4	H-H. Frentzen	Williams Renault	1'18"464
5	D. Coulthard	McLaren Mercedes	1'18"466
6	G. Fisichella	Jordan Peugeot	1'18"750

etc.

Fastest lap: D. Coulthard (McLaren Mercedes) in 1'19"635

Race result:

1	M. Schumacher	Ferrari	in 1h 17'40"646
2	J. Alesi	Benetton Renault	+2"565
3	G. Fisichella	Jordan Peugeot	+3"219
4	H-H. Frentzen	Williams Renault	+3"768
5	J. Herbert	Sauber Petronas	+4"716
6	S. Nakano	Prost Mugen Honda	+6"701
7	D. Coulthard	McLaren Mercedes	+37"753
8	P. Diniz	Arrows Yamaha	+1 lap
9	D. Hill	Arrows Yamaha	+1 lap
10	G. Morbidelli	Sauber Petronas	+1 lap
11	O. Panis	Prost Mugen Honda	+1 lap

CANADIAN GP Winners

1997 : M. SCHUMACHER (Ferrari)
1996 : D HILL (Williams)
1995 : J. ALESI (Ferrari)
1994 : M. SCHUMACHER (Benetton)

1993 : A. PROST (Williams)
1992 : G. BERGER (McLaren)
1991 : N. PIQUET (Benetton)
1990 : A. SENNA (McLaren) etc.

Nelson PIQUET is the only man to have won three Canadian GPs, in 1982-84-91. Jack BRABHAM (Brabham Repco) won the inaugural Canadian GP on 27 August 1967.

Grand Prix de France

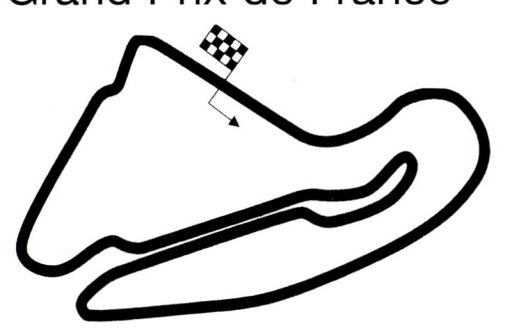

French Grand Prix

Magny-Cours

SUNDAY 28 JUNE 1998

ADDRESS: Circuit de Magny-Cours
Technopole
58470 MAGNY-COURS
FRANCE

Tel:
03 86 21 00 00
Fax:
03 86 21 8080

The circuit is 250 kilometres south of Paris, 12 to the south of Nevers and 220 north of Lyon - but it's not too far from the Swiss or German borders. Given the current passion for F1 in Michael Schumacher's homeland, that's no bad thing for the accountants at Magny-Cours. The track and the whole infrastructure are certainly amongst the best of their kind. The only drawback is the shortage of hotels in the region - and the few nearby are expensive. To get around this little problem, you can find local lodgings. But it can be costly, a kick in the teeth for the famous advertising slogan: 'France, the land of welcome'. It's bordering on a rip-off.

The years pass but some things never change. In 1998, thanks to the thorny old issue of TV rights and money, the fate of the race once again is in the hands of parliament and the governement. Even if this time good sense prevails in the end, every season the sport sails dangerously close to the wind.

START TIME: 14.00 (13.00 in Britain), 72 laps of a 4.250 km circuit, a total distance of 306.000 km.

CROWD FIGURES IN 1997: 100,000 spectators

DAVID COULTHARD'S VIEW OF *MAGNY-COURS* :

'The last corner before the pits is ridiculous compared to the rest of the track. It is bizarre, far too tight and twisty and the sort of corner that should be outlawed. The rest of the track is not too bad with some good corner sequences and a decent level of grip. The area isn't the greatest in the world but the locals are friendly. It's just a race like any other.'

French Grand Prix 1997

Starting grid:

1	M. Schumacher	Ferrari	1'14"548
2	H-H. Frentzen	Williams Renault	1'14"749
3	R. Schumacher	Jordan Peugeot	1'14"755
4	J. Villeneuve	Williams Renault	1'14"800
5	E. Irvine	Ferrari	1'14"860
6	J. Trulli	Prost Mugen Honda	1'14"957
etc.			

Fastest lap: M. Schumacher (Ferrari) in 1'17"910

Race result:

1	M. Schumacher	Ferrari	in 1h 38'50"492
2	H-H. Frentzen	Williams Renault	+23"537
3	E. Irvine	Ferrari	+1'14"801
4	J. Villeneuve	Williams Renault	+1'21"784
5	J. Alesi	Benetton Renault	+1'22"735
6	R. Schumacher	Jordan Peugeot	+1'29"871
7	D. Coulthard	McLaren Mercedes	+1 lap
8	J. Herbert	Sauber Petronas	+1 lap
9	G. Fisichella	Jordan Peugeot	+1 lap
10	J. Trulli	Prost Mugen Honda	+1 lap
11	U. Katayama	Minardi Hart	+2 laps
12	D. Hill	Arrows Yamaha	+3 laps

FRENCH GP Winners

1997 : M. SCHUMACHER (Ferrari)
1996 : D. HILL (Williams)
1995 : M. SCHUMACHER (Benetton)
1994 : M. SCHUMACHER (Benetton)

1993 : A. PROST (Williams)
1992 : N. MANSELL (Williams)
1991 : N. MANSELL (Williams)
1990 : A. PROST (Ferrari)   etc.

Alain PROST has been the most successful driver in France, winning his home race six times (81-83-88-89-90-93). Juan Manuel FANGIO (Alfa Romeo) was the winner of the first world championship Grand Prix in France, on 2 July 1950.

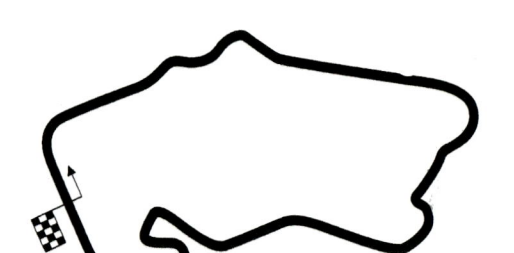

British Grand Prix
Silverstone

SUNDAY 12 JULY 1998

ADDRESS: Silverstone Circuits Ltd
Silverstone near Towcester
Northamptonshire NN12 8TN
ENGLAND

Tel:
00 44 327 85 72 71
Fax:
00 44 327 85 76 63

The self-styled 'Home of Motor Racing' lies 70 miles to the north of London, 15 south-east of Northampton and 28 from Oxford. It's a fact that, with a few notable exceptions, the majority of Formula One teams are based more or less within striking distance of London. Here, motor racing is a passion, a vocation.

The fanatics will turn out in any weather (it is often wet and always swept by a chill wind), kicking their heels for days on end just to catch a glimpse of their heroes. At Grand Prix time, almost 100,000 flock to this converted RAF aerodrome. Some of the original flavour of the track has been removed in recent years. In the interest of safety, certain areas have been reprofiled to cut cornering speeds.

The one dark shadow over Silverstone is the traffic chaos on a Sunday evening. The main access road is a complete nightmare. The best plan is to remain in the paddock for a few hours after the race, to appreciate the musical ability of Eddie Jordan, Damon Hill and Johnny Herbert, among others, in an impromptu rock concert.

START TIME: 14.00, 61 laps of a 5.143 km circuit, a total distance of 309.292 km.

CROWD FIGURES IN 1997: 90,000 spectators

DAVID COULTHARD'S VIEW OF
SILVERSTONE :
'The track has changed a lot in recent years and it has become less interesting. Sure, there are some good sequences of quick corners but I am not a fan of the new twisty bit. There is always a very good atmosphere at Silverstone and it's nice to race in front of your home crowd. That said, there are other races I prefer because there is less pressure. You can't move at Silverstone without being in demand. You talk to the fans, but I'm not sure that helps you focus your mind on the race.'

British Grand Prix 1997

Starting grid:

1	J. Villeneuve	Williams Renault	1'21"598
2	H-H. Frentzen	Williams Renault	1'21"732
3	M. Hakkinen	McLaren Mercedes	1'21"797
4	M. Schumacher	Ferrari	1'21"977
5	R. Schumacher	Jordan Peugeot	1'22"277
6	D.Coulthard	McLaren Mercedes	1'22"279
etc.			

Fastest lap: M. Schumacher (Ferrari) in 1'24"475

Race result:

1	J. Villeneuve	Williams Renault	in 1h 28'01"665
2	J. Alesi	Benetton Renault	+10"205
3	A. Wurz	Benetton Renault	+11"296
4	D. Coulthard	McLaren Mercedes	+31"229
5	R. Schumacher	Jordan Peugeot	+31"880
6	D. Hill	Arrows Yamaha	+1'13"552
7	G. Fisichella	Jordan Peugeot	+1 lap
8	J. Trulli	Prost Mugen Honda	+1 lap
9	N. Fontana	Sauber Petronas	+1 lap
10	T. Marques	Minardi Hart	+1 lap
11	S. Nakano	Prost Mugen Honda	+1 lap

BRITISH GP Winners

1997 : J. VILLENEUVE (Williams)
1996 : J. VILLENEUVE (Williams)
1995 : J. HERBERT (Benetton)
1994 : D. HILL (Williams)
1993 : A. PROST (Williams)
1992 : N. MANSELL (Williams)

1991 : N. MANSELL (Williams)
1990 : A. PROST (Ferrari)   etc.

Alain PROST (1983-85-89-90-93) and
Jim CLARK (1962-63-64-65 -67) share
the record of five wins in this event.

On 13 May 1950 Silverstone staged the very first world championship race, won by Nino FARINA (Alfa Romeo).

Grosser Preis von Oesterreich

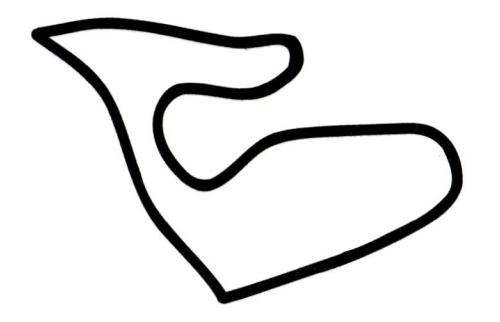

Austrian Grand Prix
A-1 Zeltweg
OSTERREICHRING

SUNDAY 26 JULY 1998

ADDRESS: A-1 Ring,
A 8724 Spielberg, AUSTRIA

Tel:
00 43 35 77 22 928
Fax:
00 43 35 77 22 928 13

Located 200 kilometres to the west of Vienna and about 100 from Graz, the verdant home of the Austrian Grand Prix was deprived of F1 for a full 10 years. Local boy Gerhard Berger fought incessantly to have his home race reinstated in the heart of the Styrian foothills, amongst the fir forests and grazing pastures. His mission accomplished, he promptly announced his retirement, passing his mantle to bright young compatriot Alexander Wurz.
The original circuit was widened and shortened, the pits were rebuilt and gravel traps were installed. As a result, the A1-Ring now looks like a modern racetrack. Here, board and lodgings are an institution, because hotels in the area are few and far between.
In the old days, this race used to be known as the holiday Grand Prix. After its return to the calendar late last September - which was miraculously sunny - it regains its traditional summer slot this season. At that time of the year, it is worth going out of your way just to be at the gateway to the Tyrolean mountains.

START TIME: 14.00 (13.00 in Britain), 71 laps of a 4.318 km circuit, a total distance of 306.578 km.

CROWD FIGURES IN 1997: 108,000 spectators

DAVID COULTHARD'S VIEW OF
ZELTWEG :
'Contrary to what you might think, this is quite a quick track, the third one of the year. Last year there wasn't much in the way of grip but it is quite easy to overtake. There was a good crowd, it is a beautiful part of the world and it is a good weekend.'

Austrian Grand Prix 1997

Starting grid:

1	J. Villeneuve	Williams Renault	1'10"304
2	M. Hakkinen	McLaren Mercedes	1'10"398
3	J. Trulli	Prost Mugen Honda	1'10"511
4	H-H. Frentzen	Williams Renault	1'10"670
5	R. Barrichello	Stewart Ford	1'10"700
6	J. Magnussen	Stewart Ford	1'10"893

etc.

Fastest lap: J. Villeneuve (Williams Renault) in 1'11"814

Race result:

1	J. Villeneuve	Williams Renault	in 1h 27'35"999
2	D. Coulthard	McLaren Mercedes	+2"909
3	H-H. Frentzen	Williams Renault	+3"962
4	G. Fisichella	Jordan Peugeot	+12"127
5	R. Schumacher	Jordan Peugeot	+31"859
6	M. Schumacher	Ferrari	+33"410
7	D. Hill	Arrows Yamaha	+37"207
8	J. Herbert	Sauber Petronas	+49"057
9	G. Morbidelli	Sauber Petronas	+1'06"406
10	G. Berger	Benetton Renault	+1 lap
11	U. Katayama	Minardi Hart	+2 laps
12	J. Verstappen	Tyrrell Ford	+2 laps
13	P. Diniz	Arrows Yamaha	+3 laps
14	R. Barrichello	Stewart Ford	+3 laps

AUSTRIAN GP Winners

1997 : J. VILLENEUVE (Williams)
1987 : N. MANSELL (Williams)
1986 : A. PROST (McLaren)
1985 : A. PROST (McLaren)
1984 : N. LAUDA (McLaren)

1983 : A. PROST (Renault)
1982 : E. DE ANGELIS (Lotus)
1981 : J. LAFFITE (Ligier)
1980 : J.P. JABOUILLE (Renault)

Alain PROST won the Austrian GP three times (1983-85-86).
The first Austrian GP winner was Lorenzo BANDINI (Ferrari), on 23 August 1964 at the Zeltweg airfield which is close to the current track.

German Grand Prix
Hockenheim

Grosser Preiss von Deutschland

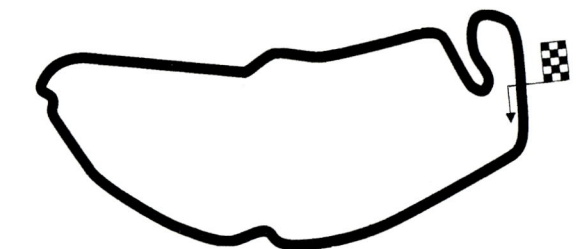

SUNDAY 2 AUGUST 1998

ADDRESS: Hockenheim Ring
Gmbh Motodrom
68766 HOCKENHEIM, GERMANY

Tel:
00 49 62 05 95 00
Fax:
00 49 62 05 95 02 99

To be found 90 kilometres south of Frankfurt, 110 north of Stuttgart and around 20 from the delightful city of Heidelberg, the circuit of Hockenheim is the only one of its kind. It's as though they have built an F1 track in the middle of a vast stadium. The huge grandstands hold around 80,000 people, each and every one devoted heart and soul to Michael Schumacher, their very own 'Schumy' who has brought them two world titles.
Thousands of German flags wave and firecrackers explode every time he goes by. The presence of his younger brother Ralf and Heinz-Harald Frentzen sets pulses racing even more around the track. Beer is quaffed as enthusiastically in the stands as it is in the camp sites which surround the circuit. Several kilometres of sausages try in vain to stem the tide. Getting up on Sunday morning is not always easy. It's a bit like a Munich beer festival, but in the absence of any Bavarian music you'll settle for a harmonious V10 symphony in C minor.
If you enjoy life taken to extremes, Hockenheim will welcome you with open arms.

START TIME: 14.00 (13.00 in Britain), 45 laps of a 6.823 km circuit, a total distance of 307.022 km.

CROWD FIGURES IN 1997: 139,000 spectators

DAVID COULTHARD'S VIEW OF *HOCKENHEIM*:

'It's incredible. You come out of the forest and into this wall of humanity before returning to the woods for a minute and a half, back on your own amid calm. In the middle of the fir trees there are a few chicanes but there's no-one watching out there. There is nowhere else like Hockenheim. The crowd is enthusiastic and I like it.'

German Grand Prix 1997

Starting grid:

1	G. Berger	Benetton Renault	1'41"873
2	G. Fisichella	Jordan Peugeot	1'41"896
3	M. Hakkinen	McLaren Mercedes	1'42"034
4	M. Schumacher	Ferrari	1'42"181
5	H.H. Frentzen	Williams Renault	1'42"421
6	J. Alesi	Benetton Renault	1'42"493

etc.

Fastest lap: G. Berger (Benetton Renault) in 1'45"747

Race result:

1	G. Berger	Benetton Renault	in 1h20'59"046
2	M. Schumacher	Ferrari	+17"527
3	M. Hakkinen	McLaren Mercedes	+24"770
4	J. Trulli	Prost Mugen Honda	+27"165
5	R. Schumacher	Jordan Peugeot	+29"995
6	J. Alesi	Benetton Renault	+34"717
7	S. Nakano	Prost Mugen Honda	+1'19"722
8	D. Hill	Arrows Yamaha	+1 lap
9	J. Verstappen	Tyrrell Ford	+1 lap
10	G. Fisichella	Jordan Peugeot	+3 laps

GERMAN GP Winners

1997 : G. BERGER (Benetton)
1996 : D. HILL (Williams)
1995 : M. SCHUMACHER (Benetton)
1994 : G. BERGER (Ferrari)
1993 : A. PROST (Williams)
1992 : N. MANSELL (Williams)
1991 : N. MANSELL (Williams)
1990 : A. SENNA (McLaren)   etc.

Juan Manuel FANGIO (1954-56-57), Nelson PIQUET (1981-86-87) and Ayrton SENNA (1988-89-90) all have three victories in the German GP. Alberto ASCARI (Alfa Romeo) was the first to win a world championship GP in Germany, at the Nürburgring on 29 July 1951.

Hungarian Grand Prix
Hungaroring Budapest

Magyar Nagyij

SUNDAY 16 AUGUST 1998

ADDRESS: Magyar Auto es
Motorsport Szöversteg
Dozsa Gyorgy Str. 1-3
1143 BUDAPEST, HUNGARY

Tel:
00 36 61 115 84 69
Fax:
00 36 61 163 34 67

The track lies close to the small town of Mogyorod, about 20 kilometres north-east of Budapest. When the venue opened in 1986, the admission prices were very low. Still behind the Iron Curtain at the time, the Hungarians responded en masse to the lure of capitalism. As the years rolled on and inflation took its grip, the cost of tickets rose beyond the means of local enthusiasts.

It was said that the cost of admission equated to a month's salary. Coincidentally, this period of transition coincided with the growth in stature of Michael Schumacher, as a result of which hordes of Germans and Austrians snapped up grandstand seats. This imported affluence has assured the survival of the event, although the effect of Gerhard Berger's retirement might be felt at the ticket kiosks.

The weather is particularly good at race time and the verdant setting makes this a very pleasant weekend. Budapest being such a wonderful city, it makes sense to capitalise on the chance to take a short pre-race holiday, drifting down the Danube to a backdrop of Bohemian music.

START TIME: 14.00 (3.00 in Britain), 77 laps of a 3.968 km circuit, a total distance of 305.536 km.

CROWD FIGURES IN 1997: 120,000 spectators

DAVID COULTHARD'S VIEW OF BUDAPEST:

'I don't like it much. The Hungarians are charming people but I can't say the same for their racetrack. It is far too slow and twisty and there isn't much grip. Enough said. It is my least favourite race of the season.'

Statistiques du GP de Hongrie 1997

Starting grid:

1	M. Schumacher	Ferrari	1'14"672
2	J. Villeneuve	Williams Renault	1'14"859
3	D. Hill	Arrows Yamaha	1'15"044
4	M. Hakkinen	McLaren Mercedes	1'15"140
5	E. Irvine	Ferrari	1'15"424
6	H-H. Frentzen	Williams Renault	1'15"520

etc.

Fastest lap: H-H. Frentzen (Williams Renault) in 1'18"372

Race result:

1	J. Villeneuve	Williams Renault	in 1h 45'47"149
2	D. Hill	Arrows Yamaha	+9"079
3	J. Herbert	Sauber Petronas	+20"445
4	M. Schumacher	Ferrari	+30"501
5	R. Schumacher	Jordan Peugeot	+30"715
6	S. Nakano	Prost Mugen Honda	+41"512
7	J. Trulli	Prost Mugen Honda	+1'15"552
8	G. Berger	Benetton Renault	+1'16"409
9	E. Irvine	Ferrari	+1 lap
10	U. Katayama	Minardi Hart	+1 lap
11	J. Alesi	Benetton Renault	+1 lap
12	T. Marques	Minardi Hart	+2 laps
13	M. Salo	Tyrrell Ford	+2 laps

HUNGARIAN GP Winners

1997 : J. VILLENEUVE (Williams)
1996 : J. VILLENEUVE (Williams)
1995 : D. HILL (Williams)
1994 : M. SCHUMACHER (Benetton)

1993 : D. HILL (Williams)
1992 : A. SENNA (McLaren)
1991 : A. SENNA (McLaren)
1990 : T. BOUTSEN (Williams)

Ayrton SENNA won this race three times (1988-91-92).
Nelson PIQUET was the winner of the inaugural Hungarian GP, on 10 August 1986.

Grand Prix de Belgique

Belgian Grand Prix
Spa-Francorchamps
SUNDAY 24 AUGUST 1998

ADDRESS: Circuit de Spa-Francorchamps
Route du circuit 55
4970 FRANCORCHAMPS
BELGIUM

Tel:
00 32 87 27 52 58
Fax:
00 32 87 27 52 96

Fifty kilometres to the south-east of Liège and to the south-west of the German town of Aachen, the circuit's place in the world championship has been threatened by the laws against tobacco advertising. Spa-Francorchamps was only reinstated in the calendar in mid-February. For many German fans, Spa is actually the closest race to home. That's another reason for Michael Schumacher to feel especially at home in the Ardennes, at the track where he both made his F1 début and scored his first Grand Prix win. His compatriots arrive in their tens of thousands to cheer him on - and they don't forget to bring their macs and umbrellas. As the summer draws to a close, this region is especially prone to rain. That's a shame, because this is a magnificent setting ... when it's sunny! The circuit is one of the remaining links with the sport's glorious past. Although some of its legendary corners are no longer there, it remains one of the favourite tracks of all Grand Prix drivers. The local people are friendly, the food is good and the hotels are comfortable. But watch out for the speed traps! It would be a shame to tarnish such a splendid weekend.

START TIME: 14.00 (13.00 in Britain), 44 laps of a 6.968 km circuit, a total distance of 306.592 km.

CROWD FIGURES IN 1997: 80,000 spectators

DAVID COULTHARD'S VIEW OF SPA:

'It's my favourite track of the year. The corners are fast and flowing, the circuit rises and falls ... Unfortunately the weather is not always brilliant and you are a long way from the public. It's difficult to strike up a rapport with the crowd like you can at Hockenheim. But no matter what the weather, the atmosphere is always brilliant. It's the best weekend of the year.'

Belgian Grand Prix 1997

Starting grid:

1	J. Villeneuve	Williams Renault	1'49"450
2	J. Alesi	Benetton Renault	1'49"759
3	M. Schumacher	Ferrari	1'50"293
4	G. Fisichella	Jordan Peugeot	1'50"470
5	M. Hakkinen	McLaren Mercedes	1'50"503
6	R. Schumacher	Jordan Peugeot	1'50"520

etc.

Fastest lap: J. Villeneuve (Williams Renault) in 1'52"692

Race result:

1	M. Schumacher	Ferrari	in 1h 33'46"717
2	G. Fisichella	Jordan Peugeot	+26"753
3	M. Hakkinen	McLaren Mercedes	+30"856
4	H-H. Frentzen	Williams Renault	+32"147
5	J. Herbert	Sauber Petronas	+39"025
6	J. Villeneuve	Williams Renault	+42"103
7	G. Berger	Benetton Renault	+1'03"741
8	P. Diniz	Arrows Yamaha	+1'25"931
9	J. Alesi	Benetton Renault	+1'42"008
10	G. Morbidelli	Sauber Petronas	+1'42"582
11	E. Irvine	Ferrari	+1 lap
12	M. Salo	Tyrrell Ford	+1 lap
13	J. Magnussen	Stewart Ford	+1 lap
14	D. Hill	Arrows Yamaha	+2 laps
15	U. Katayama	Minardi Hart	+2 laps
16	J. Trulli	Prost Mugen Honda	+2 laps

BELGIAN GP Winners

1997 : M. SCHUMACHER (Ferrari)
1996 : M. SCHUMACHER (Ferrari)
1995 : M. SCHUMACHER (Benetton)
1994 : D. HILL (Williams)
1993 : D. HILL (Williams)
1992 : M. SCHUMACHER (Benetton)
1991 : A. SENNA (McLaren)
1990 : A. SENNA (McLaren)

Ayrton SENNA has scored the most victories at Spa, winning five times (1985-88-89-90-91).
Jim CLARK was victorious in Belgium on four occasions (1962-63-64-65).
Juan Manuel FANGIO (Alfa Romeo) won the first Belgian GP at Spa, on 18 June 1950.

Gran Premio d'Italia

Italian Grand Prix
Monza

SUNDAY 13 SEPTEMBER 1998

ADDRESS: Autodromo Nazionale
di Monza
Parco Monza
20052 MONZA, ITALY

Tel:
00 39 39 24 821
Fax:
00 39 39 32 324

The parkland home of the Monza circuit is only 15 kilometres north-east of Milan. Along with Monaco, Silverstone, Spa and the Nürburgring, it is one of the F1 legends, one of the world championship's historic remnants.
The first Grand Prix race took place here as long ago as 1922. And even in those days, the organisers had their hands full with the local authorities, who were concerned with the protection of the park. In 1994, after the tragedies at Imola, the realignment of certain corners provoked serious disputes with the Greens.
Usually, Monza is more concerned with the Reds. When the Ferrari are competitive, the place is in uproar. When Schumacher won in 1996, the place went berserk. Bearing thousands of flags emblazoned with team colours, the jubilant tifosi invaded the circuit and crowded beneath the podium to pay a vibrant, glowing tribute to their new idol. You wouldn't see anything quite like it elsewhere; that's the magic of Monza.

START TIME: 14.00 (13.00 in Britain), 53 laps of a 5.769 km circuit, a total distance of 305.757 km.

CROWD FIGURES IN 1997: 115,000 spectators

DAVID COULTHARD'S VIEW OF *MONZA*:

'I love the atmosphere at Monza, which is dripping with history. The park itself is fabulous and I adore the Parabolica corner. Lots of people complain that there are too many straights, but that makes it difficult to balance the car, to get good straightline speed and be quick through the chicanes. It's a challenge and the tifosi are amazing. The atmosphere is always good in Italy, but I think Monza is b etter than Imola.'

Italian Grand Prix 1997

Starting grid:

1	Jean Alesi	Benetton Renault	1'22"990
2	H-H. Frentzen	Williams Renault	1'23"042
3	G. Fisichella	Jordan Peugeot	1'23"066
4	J. Villeneuve	Williams Renault	1'23"231
5	M. Hakkinen	McLaren Mercedes	1'23"340
6	D. Coulthard	McLaren Mercedes	1'23"347

etc.

Fastest lap: M. Hakkinen (McLaren Mercedes) in 1'24"808

Race result:

1	D. Coulthard	McLaren Mercedes	in 1h17'04"609
2	J. Alesi	Benetton Renault	+1"937
3	H-H. Frentzen	Williams Renault	+4"343
4	G. Fisichella	Jordan Peugeot	+5"871
5	J. Villeneuve	Williams Renault	+6"416
6	M. Schumacher	Ferrari	+11"481
7	G. Berger	Benetton Renault	+12"471
8	E. Irvine	Ferrari	+17"639
9	M. Hakkinen	McLaren Mercedes	+49"373
10	J. Trulli	Prost Mugen Honda	+1'02"706
11	S. Nakano	Prost Mugen Honda	+1'03"727
12	G. Morbidelli	Sauber Petronas	+1 lap
13	R. Barrichello	Stewart Ford	+1 lap
14	T. Marques	Minardi Hart	+3 laps

ITALIAN GP Winners

1997 : D. COULTHARD (McLaren)
1996 : M. SCHUMACHER (Ferrari)
1995 : J. HERBERT (Benetton)
1994 : D. HILL (Williams)
1993 : D. HILL (Williams)
1992 : A. SENNA (McLaren)
1991 : N. MANSELL (Williams)

1990 : A. SENNA (McLaren)

Nelson PIQUET has won this race four times (1980-83-86-87).

No fewer than four drivers have won it three times each: Juan Manuel FANGIO (1953-54-55); Stirling MOSS (1956-57-59); Ronnie PETERSON (1973-74-76); and Alain PROST (1981-85- 89).

The first Italian GP counting towards the world championship was won by Giuseppe FARINA (Alfa Romeo), on 3 September 1950.

Luxembourg Grand Prix
Nürburgring

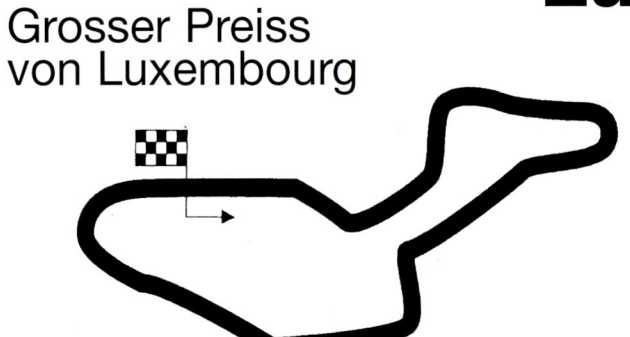

Grosser Preiss von Luxembourg

SUNDAY 27 SEPTEMBER 1998

ADDRESS:
Nürburgring Gmbh
53520 Nürburg / Eifel
GERMANY

Tel:
00 49 26 91 30 20
Fax:
00 49 26 91 302 155

Sixty kilometres to the east of Koblenz, 80 to the south of Cologne and 55 from Bonn, the famous Nürburgring was originally built by the Third Reich in the shadow of the mysterious castle ruins at Nürburg.
Used by F1 until Niki Lauda's terrible accident in 1976, this legendary circuit from a bygone age measured 22.835 kilometres - the race lasted only 14 laps! To get a taste of those days, you can take your own car around the old circuit for around DM20 per lap. It's an open air museum of sorts. As the national GP switched to Hockenheim, the organisers decided to build a new Nürburgring, retaining only the original pit straight.
In 1984, the Grand Prix of Europe took place at the brand new circuit, whose vast grandstands give it a stadium appearance. Thanks to the F1 craze sweeping Germany at present, the grandstands are filled to bursting point. It's just a shame that the weather in the Eifel mountains is not always clement, particularly at the beginning of autumn.

START TIME: 14.00 (13.00 in Britain), 67 laps of a 4.556 km circuit, a total distance of 305.252 km.

CROWD FIGURES IN 1997: 108,000 spectators

DAVID COULTHARD'S VIEW OF *NÜRBURGRING*:
'It is a modern circuit in the vein of Barcelona and Magny-Cours, without a great deal of character. It is not terribly long, but the chicanes and corners have been well executed. There's plenty of grip and overtaking is not too difficult. Unfortunately, it always seems to be cold when we go there.'

Luxembourg Grand Prix 1997

Starting grid:

1	M. Hakkinen	McLaren Mercedes	1'16"602
2	J. Villeneuve	Williams Renault	1'16"691
3	H-H. Frentzen	Williams Renault	1'16"741
4	G. Fisichella	Jordan Peugeot	1'17"289
5	M. Schumacher	Ferrari	1'17"385
6	D. Coulthard	McLaren Mercedes	1'17"387

etc.

Race result:

1	J. Villeneuve	Williams Renault	in 1h 31"27"843
2	J. Alesi	Benetton Renault	+11"770
3	H-H. Frentzen	Williams Renault	+13"480
4	G. Berger	Benetton Renault	+16"416
5	P. Diniz	Arrows Yamaha	+43"147
6	O. Panis	Prost Mugen Honda	+43"593
7	J. Herbert	Sauber Petronas	+44"354
8	D. Hill	Arrows Yamaha	+44"777
9	G. Morbidelli	Sauber Petronas	+1 lap
10	M. Salo	Tyrrell Ford	+1 lap

Fastest lap: H-H. Frentzen (Williams Renault) in 1'18"805

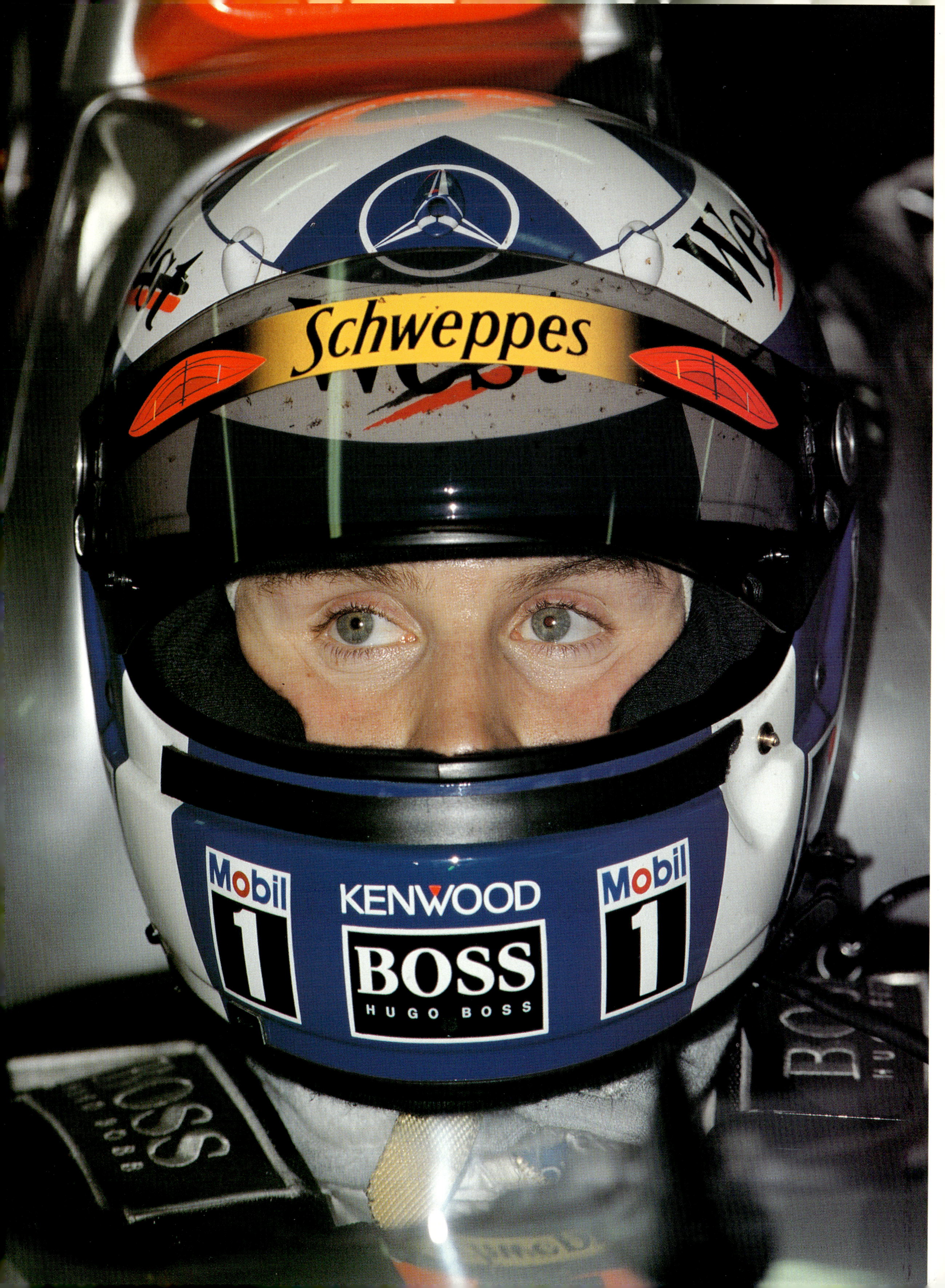
Schweppes
Mobil
1
KENWOOD
BOSS
HUGO BOSS
Mobil
1

Japanese Grand Prix
SUZUKA
SUNDAY 12 OCTOBER 1998

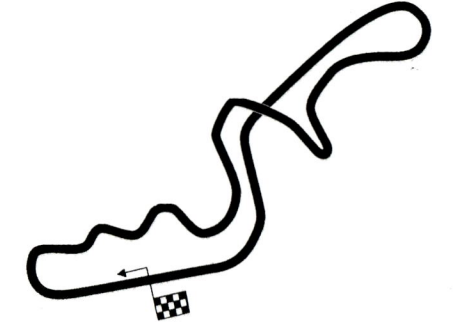

ADDRESS:
Suzuka circuit GP Office
7992 Ino-Cho, Suzuka,
Mie-Ken 510-02
JAPAN

Tel:
00 81 593 70 14 65
Fax:
00 81 593 70 18 18

The circuit takes some getting to. It is 500 kilometres west of Tokyo, 150 east of Osaka and 70 south-west of Nagoya. You have to tackle something of an assault course to reach the Honda leisure park which houses the Suzuka circuit. It is a totally disorientating experience. Even if interest in Formula One has diminished locally since the death of the revered Ayrton Senna, the Japanese nonetheless flock to the venue in droves. They even sleep on site in order to grab the best view the following morning. It is still a sell-out, but it is no longer necessary to hold a lottery to decide which fortunate applicants could spend a fortune to secure their seat.

Honda is contemplating an official return to F1 and is laying the groundwork to regain its former position of eminence within the sport. And for his part, former star driver Satoru Nakajima has been working with Tyrrell to boost national fortunes in F1. There are new Japanese drivers on the way.

START TIME: 14.00 (05.00 in Britain), 53 laps of a 5.864 circuit, a total distance of 310.792 km.

CROWD FIGURES IN 1997: 140,000 spectators

DAVID COULTHARD'S VIEW OF SUZUKA:

'It's a very demanding circuit, like Spa. There is a good mixture of fast and slow corners. I enjoy the atmosphere and I don't have any problem with the locals' fanaticism. There's always a huge crowd because F1 is enormously popular over there.'

Japanese Grand Prix 1997

Starting grid:
1. J. Villeneuve (Williams)   1'36"071
2. M. Schumacher (Ferrari)   1'36"133
3. E. Irvine (Ferrari)   1'36"466
4. M. Hakkinen (McLaren)   1'36"469
5. G. Berger (Benetton)   1'36"561
6. H-H. Frentzen (Williams)   1'36"628
etc.

Fastest lap: H-H. Frentzen (Williams) in 1'38"942

Race result
1. M. Schumacher (Ferrari)   in 1h 29'48"446
2. H-H. Frentzen (Williams)   +1"378
3. E. Irvine (Ferrari)   +26"384
4. M. Hakkinen (McLaren)   +27"129
5. J. Alesi (Benetton)   +40"403
6. J. Herbert (Sauber)   +41"630
7. G. Fisichella (Jordan)   +58'825
8. G. Berger (Benetton)   +1'00"429
9. R. Schumacher (Jordan)   +1'22"036
10. D. Coulthard (McLaren)   +1 lap
11. D. Hill (Arrows)   +1 lap
12. P. Diniz (Arrows)   +1 lap
13. J. Verstappen (Tyrrell)   +1 lap

JAPANESE GP Winners

1997 : M. SCHUMACHER (Ferrari)
1996 : D. HILL (Williams)
1995 : M. SCHUMACHER (Ferrari)
1994 : D. HILL (Williams)
1993 : A. SENNA (McLaren)
1992 : N. MANSELL (Williams)
1991 : G. BERGER (McLaren)
1990 : N. PIQUET (Benetton)

Four drivers have won the Japanese GP twice each: Gerhard BERGER (1987-91), Ayrton SENNA (1988-93), Damon HILL (1994-96) and Michael SCHUMACHER (1995-97).

The first Japanese GP took place at Mount Fuji on 24 October 1976 and was won by Mario ANDRETTI (Lotus)

The Changes for 1998

More than ever, safety is the prime concern. F1's rule-makers are constantly trying to find stop-gap measures to curb performance gains.

The arrival of Bridgestone in 1997 relaunched Grand Prix racing's tyre war. Circuit statistics show that qualifying times in 1997 were three to four seconds faster per lap than in the previous year. It was time for the FIA's technical team to act. The new rules are based on six fundamental points: tyres, brakes, monocoque, cockpit size, narrow track suspension and wing dimensions.

Tyres: This is the most radical of the new rules. The appearance of obligatory grooves (three at the front and four at the rear) will guarantee a reduction in grip and make cars less stable. It marks the end for the formidably efficient slick tyres.

Having tried the new tyres at the start of the summer, world champion Jacques Villeneuve voiced strong opposition to this change. The FIA were less than appreciative of his comments and summoned him to Paris for a dressing down. Four days before his home Grand Prix in Canada, Villeneuve suggested that he might be forced to pursue his career on the other side of the Atlantic!

Brakes: In an attempt to encourage overtaking on the track rather than as a result of pit stops, the legislators have reduced the thickness and diameter of the discs. The calipers are made of aluminium, with no more than two pads per caliper. This restrictive measure will make braking distances longer. Overtaking, the true essence of motor racing, will again become the order of the day.

The monocoque: In order to ensure better leg protection for drivers, the top of the monocoque is now 350mm from the front wheel axis, rather than 250mm. Crash-tests will also be more severe this year.

The cockpit: As the goal is always to increase safety, cockpits will be less enclosed, to facilitate a quick escape in the event of an accident. The height of the cockpit sides will also be increased to improve drivers' head protection.

Narrower track: In order to keep performance in check, cars have been reduced from a maximum width of 2 metres to 1.8 metres. This common sense measure will lessen the aggressive stance of 1998's Formula One cars. The man-in-the-street could even confuse them for Formula Three machines fitted with oversize tyres. These new procedures are designed to reduce braking and cornering efficiency.

The wings: While the cockpit area has grown in size, wings have been made smaller. Like the narrower track measurement, this will also reduce a car's stability on the racing circuit.

Through these measures, the governing body hopes that its preoccupation with greater safety will have an added bonus in the form of an improved spectacle. From grandstand or TV armchair, the public will witness the end of the era in which cars have been glued to the ground. There should be more overtaking on the track and cars will slide around more. It promises to be the best of both worlds, and worldwide TV audiences should swell as a result.

F1 facts and figures
test your motor racing memory

The 1998 Australian Grand Prix is the 615th race in world championship history.
How many of the following could you have answered?

The longest race in world championship history?
The Indianapolis 500 (805 km, 1950-60).
The shortest race in world championship history?
Australia 1991 (53 km).
The most time-consuming race in world championship history?
Indianapolis 1951 (3h 57' 38").
The briefest race in world championship history?
Australia 1991 (24'34").
The number of countries to have staged a GP?
23.
The number of circuits to have staged a GP?
58.
The fastest ever GP pole position?
258.984 km/h/160.935mph (Keke Rosberg, British GP 1985).
The fastest ever GP race average?
242.615 km/h/150.755 mph (Peter Gethin, Italian GP 1971).
The greatest winning margin?
2 laps (Spanish GP 1969, between Stewart and McLaren, and Australian GP 1995, between Hill and Panis).
The smallest winning margin?
0.010s between Gethin and Peterson at Monza in 1971.
The greatest number of starters in a GP?
34 (German GP 1953).

The smallest number of starters in a GP?
13 (Spanish GP 1968).
The highest number of recorded finishers?
22 (British GP 1952).
The lowest number of recorded finishers?
4 (Monaco GP 1966).
The most frequently used circuit?
Monza, 47 races.
The youngest driver ever to start a GP?
Mike Thackwell, 19yrs 5m 29days (Canadian GP 1980).
The oldest driver ever to start a GP?
Louis Chiron, 55yrs 9m 19days (Monaco GP 1955).
The youngest ever world championship race winner?
Troy Ruttmann, 22yrs 2m 19days (Indianapolis 500 1952).
The oldest ever world championship race winner?
Luigi Fagioli, 53yrs 0m 22days (French GP 1951).
The youngest world champion?
Emerson Fittipaldi, 25yrs 8m 29days (1972).
The oldest world champion?
Juan Manuel Fangio, 46yrs 1m 11days (1957)
The highest tally of world championship titles?
5 (Fangio).
The greatest number of GP starts?
256 (Patrese).
The record for Grand Prix victories?
51 (Prost).
The highest number of second-place finishes?
35 (Prost).
The highest number of third-place finishes?
21 (Berger).

The record number of podium finishes?
106 (Prost).
The all-time career points-scoring record?
798.5 (Prost).
The record for points in a single season?
108 (Mansell in 1992).
The record for victories in a single season?
9 (Mansell in 1992 and Schumacher in 1995).
The record for having won the same race the most times?
6 (Senna at Monaco and Prost in Brazil and France).
The greatest number of successive race wins?
9 (Ascari in 1952-53).
The greatest number of kilometres in the lead?
13,469 km (Senna).
The record number of pole positions?
65 (Senna).

The record for pole positions in one season?
14 (Mansell in 1992).
The greatest number of fastest laps?
41 (Prost).
The greatest number of fastest laps in one season?
8 (Mansell in 1992).
The country with the greatest number of GP successes?
Great Britain, 173 wins by 16 drivers
The most successful manufacturer in terms of wins?
Ferrari, 113.
The record for world constructors' championships?
9 (Williams).
The record number of points by a team in a single season?
199 (McLaren in 1988).
The highest number of points scored by a team from 1950-1997?
2093.5 (Ferrari).
The record number of victories for one team in a season?
15 (McLaren in 1988).

The record number of one-two finishes?
40 (Ferrari).
The record number of one-two finishes in one season?
10 (McLaren in 1988).
The team with the most pole positions?
Ferrari, 121.
The team with the most pole positions in a season?
McLaren, 15 in 1988-89 and Williams in 1992-93.
The team record for the highest number of victories at the same circuit?
11 (Ferrari at Monza).
The most successful engine supplier?
Ford, 174 wins.
The highest number of wins by the same engine in one season?
16 (Renault in 1995).
The highest number of pole positions by an engine?
138 (Ford).
The highest number of pole positions in one season by an engine?
16 (Renault in 1995).

The Cost of Formula 1

Spare parts price list

	£ sterling		£ sterling
Brake pad	90	Rear wing	18,000
Steering wheel	7,000	Deformable fuel tank	6,000
Wing mirror	300	Engine cover	5,500
Tyre (each)	350	Floor	5,500
Wheel	400	Exhaust	2,500
Brake disc	700	Front suspension	35,000
Suspension wishbone	1,350	Rear suspension	38,000
Shock absorber	700	Carbon monocoque	60,000
Brake caliper	3,000	Telemetry system	90,000
Pedal assembly	6,300	Gearbox and transmission	70,000
Steering system	2,800	Electronic wiring loom	70,000
Dashboard	5,500	Customer engine	60,000
Nose and front wing	9,500	Works engine	200,000

NB: Tyre budget only previously concerned the smaller teams, as the big guns benefited from Goodyear's policy of free tyre supply. For the others, the purchase of tyres made up a considerable part of the total budget. The arrival of Bridgestone has changed all that. Now both tyre suppliers provide their goods free of charge. That is a real godsend for the second division teams.

Engine budget is a major part of the expense equation for some.
Mecachrome, which has taken over servicing Renault's old V10s, will bill its customers Williams and Benetton £10 million each for the season.

The Ford Zetec engine used by Tyrrell and Minardi is more affordable, the cost per annum being around £4 million.

The teams' Formula One budgets in 1998

Only Prost Grand Prix has given an official figure for its racing budget in 1998. The rest have been calculated on the basis of combining known facts with unofficial information from sources within the teams.

	£sterling
Ferrari	90,000,000
McLaren	90,000,000
Williams	55,000,000
Benetton	35,000,000
Prost	30,000,000
Sauber	30,000,000
Jordan	30,000,000
Arrows	25,000,000
Stewart	20,000,000
Tyrrell	20,000,000
Minardi	13,000,000

NB: Approximately one-third of the teams' budgets comes from money accrued by TV rights. This is distributed according to a secret calculation made by Formula One Administration (FOA) in respect of performance and organisers' prize funds. In 1997 McLaren, Williams and Tyrrell refused to sign the Concorde Agreement which controls these rights and they were thus ineligible for this sizeable windfall. This year every team has returned to the fold. It is reasonable to estimate that Williams will accrue about £20 million from TV rights - roughly the entire seasonal budget of some smaller teams.

The drivers' annual salaries

Working out the drivers' pay packets requires even more detective work than it does to calculate the teams' budgets. These salary figures do not take into account win bonuses or advertising contracts. To take Michael Schumacher as an example, his product endorsements could allow him to double his income. As a result, he might accrue enough to run a middle-ranking F1 team such as Prost or Jordan.

	£sterling
M. Schumacher	15,000,000
J. Villeneuve	7,200,000
D. Hill	6,000,000
H.H. Frentzen	3,000,000
J. Alesi	3,000,000
E. Irvine	3,000,000
M. Hakkinen	2,400,000
D. Coulthard	2,400,000
O. Panis	1,200,000
J. Herbert	1,200,000
G. Fisichella	1,200,000
etc ...	

Although the amount can vary from Grand Prix to Grand Prix, race organisers receive a bill from FOCA for approximately £5 million for the right to stage a Formula One race.

The cost of Formula 1

Statistics

Drivers

The 46 world champions

1950	Giuseppe FARINA	(ITALY)	ALFA ROMEO
1951	Juan Manuel FANGIO	(ARGENTINA)	ALFA ROMEO
1952	Alberto ASCARI	(ITALY)	FERRARI
1953	Alberto ASCARI	(ITALY)	FERRARI
1954	Juan Manuel FANGIO	(ARGENTINA)	MERCEDES & MASERATI
1955	Juan Manuel FANGIO	(ARGENTINA)	MERCEDES
1956	Juan Manuel FANGIO	(ARGENTINA)	LANCIA-FERRARI
1957	Juan Manuel FANGIO	(ARGENTINA)	MASERATI
1958	Mike HAWTHORN	(GREAT BRITAIN)	FERRARI
1959	Jack BRABHAM	(AUSTRALIA)	COOPER CLIMAX
1960	Jack BRABHAM	(AUSTRALIA)	COOPER CLIMAX
1961	Phil HILL	(UNITED STATES)	FERRARI
1962	Graham HILL	(GREAT BRITAIN)	BRM
1963	Jim CLARK	(GREAT BRITAIN)	LOTUS CLIMAX
1964	John SURTEES	(GREAT BRITAIN)	FERRARI
1965	Jim CLARK	(GREAT BRITAIN)	LOTUS CLIMAX
1966	Jack BRABHAM	(AUSTRALIA)	BRABHAM REPCO
1967	Denis HULME	(NEW ZEALAND)	BRABHAM REPCO
1968	Graham HILL	GREAT BRITAIN)	LOTUS FORD
1969	Jackie STEWART	(GREAT BRITAIN)	MATRA FORD
1970	Jochen RINDT	(AUSTRIA)	LOTUS FORD
1971	Jackie STEWART	(GREAT BRITAIN)	TYRRELL FORD
1972	Emerson FITTIPALDI	(BRAZIL)	LOTUS FORD
1973	Jackie STEWART	(GREAT BRITAIN)	TYRRELL FORD
1974	Emerson FITTIPALDI	(BRAZIL)	McLAREN FORD
1975	Niki LAUDA	(AUSTRIA)	FERRARI
1976	James HUNT	(GREAT BRITAIN)	McLAREN FORD
1977	Niki LAUDA	(AUSTRIA)	FERRARI
1978	Mario ANDRETTI	(UNITED STATES)	LOTUS FORD
1979	Jody SCHECKTER	(SOUTH AFRICA)	FERRARI
1980	Alan JONES	(AUSTRALIA)	WILLIAMS FORD
1981	Nelson PIQUET	(BRAZIL)	BRABHAM FORD
1982	Keke ROSBERG	(FINLAND)	WILLIAMS FORD
1983	Nelson PIQUET	(BRAZIL)	BRABHAM BMW
1984	Niki LAUDA	(AUSTRIA)	McLAREN TAG PORSCHE
1985	Alain PROST	(FRANCE)	McLAREN TAG PORSCHE
1986	Alain PROST	(FRANCE)	McLAREN TAG PORSCHE
1987	Nelson PIQUET	(BRAZIL)	WILLIAMS HONDA
1988	Ayrton SENNA	(BRAZIL)	McLAREN HONDA
1989	Alain PROST	(FRANCE)	McLAREN HONDA
1990	Ayrton SENNA	(BRAZIL)	McLAREN HONDA
1991	Ayrton SENNA	(BRAZIL)	McLAREN HONDA
1992	Nigel MANSELL	(GREAT BRITAIN)	WILLIAMS RENAULT
1993	Alain PROST	(FRANCE)	WILLIAMS RENAULT
1994	Michael SCHUMACHER	(GERMANY)	BENETTON FORD
1995	Michael SCHUMACHER	(GERMANY)	BENETTON RENAULT
1996	Damon HILL	(GREAT BRITAIN)	WILLIAMS RENAULT
1997	Jacques VILLENEUVE	(CANADA)	WILLIAMS RENAULT

Statistics - up to 31 December 1997 -

Constructors

In 1958, the Formula One Constructors Cup was created. In 1982 it was replaced by the Official Constructors World Championship.

1958: VANWALL	1978: LOTUS
1959: COOPER	1979: FERRARI
1960: COOPER	1980: WILLIAMS
1961: FERRARI	1981: WILLIAMS
1962: BRM	1982: FERRARI
1963: LOTUS	1983: FERRARI
1964: FERRARI	1984: McLAREN
1965: LOTUS	1985: McLAREN
1966: BRABHAM	1986: WILLIAMS
1967: BRABHAM	1987: WILLIAMS
1967: LOTUS	1988: McLAREN
1968: LOTUS	1989: McLAREN
1969: MATRA	1990: McLAREN
1970: LOTUS	1991: McLAREN
1971: TYRRELL	1992: WILLIAMS
1972: LOTUS	1993: WILLIAMS
1973: LOTUS	1994: WILLIAMS
1974: McLAREN	1995: BEN ETTON
1975: FERRARI	1996: WILLIAMS
1976: FERRARI	1997: WILLIAMS
1977: FERRARI	

Number of drivers' world championship titles by nation

12 TITLES GREAT BRITAIN: Hawthorn (1), G. Hill (2), Clark (2), Surtees (1), Stewart (3), HUNT (1), Mansell (1), D. Hill (1)

8 TITLES BRAZIL: E. Fittipaldi (2), Piquet(3), Senna (3)

5 TITLES ARGENTINA: Fangio (5)

4 TITLES AUSTRALIA: Brabham (3), Jones (1)
AUSTRIA: Rindt (1), Lauda (3)
FRANCE: Prost (4)

3 TITLES ITALY: Farina (1), Ascari (2)

2 TITLES UNITED STATES: P.Hill (1), M.Andretti (1)
GERMANY: M. Schumacher (2)

1 TITLE NEW ZEALAND: Hulme
SOUTH AFRICA: Scheckter
FINLAND: Rosberg
CANADA: J. Villeneuve

Number of Grand Prix contested by driver

R. Patrese	256	J. Ickx	116	M. Surer	82
G. Berger	210	A. Jones	116	M. Trintignant	82
A. de Cesaris	208	K. Rosberg	114	R. Barrichello	81
N. Piquet	204	P. Tambay	114	S. Johansson	79
A. Prost	199	J. Herbert	113	A. Nannini	77
M. Alboreto	194	D. Hulme	112	P. Ghinzani	76
N. Mansell	187	J. Scheckter	112	S. Nakajima	74
G. Hill	176	J. Surtees	111	V. Brambilla	74
J. Laffite	176	E. de Angelis	108	M. Gugelmin	74
N. Lauda	171	P. Alliot	107	H-J. Stuck	74
T. Boutsen	163	J. Mass	105	J. Clark	72
A. Senna	161	J. Bonnier	102	C. Pace	72
M. Brundle	158	M. Schumacher	102	S. Modena	70
J. Watson	152	B. McLaren	101	D. Pironi	70
R. Arnoux	149	J. Stewart	99	B. Giacomelli	69
D. Warwick	147	J. Siffert	97	G. Villeneuve	67
C. Reutemann	146	C. Amon	96	S. Moss	66
E. Fittipaldi	144	M. Hakkinen	96	H-H. Frentzen	65
J-P. Jarier	135	P. Depailler	95	E. Irvine	65
J. Alesi	135	U. Katayama	95	T. Fabi	64
E. Cheever	132	I. Capelli	94	A. Suzuki	64
C. Regazzoni	132	J. Hunt	92	J.J. Lehto	62
Ma. Andretti	128	J-P. Beltoise	86	M. Blundell	61
J. Brabham	126	D. Gurney	86	G. Morbidelli	60
R. Peterson	123	J. Palmer	84	J. Rindt	60
P-L. Martini	119	D. Hill	84	etc ...	

Other drivers who contested the 1997 World Championship

O. Panis	59	J. Verstappen	48	R. Schumacher	17
D. Coulthard	58	J. Villeneuve	33	J. Trulli	14
M. Salo	52	G. Fisichella	25	T. Marques	12
P. Diniz	50	J. Magnussen	18	N. Fontana	4
N. Larini	49	S. Nakano	17	A. Wurz	3

NB: The world championship comprised fewer events from the 1950s to the 1970s, so we shouldn't forget a few famous drivers, not least five-times champion Juan Manuel Fangio, who started only 51 races!

P. Rodriguez	55	L. Bandini	42	P. Collins	32
J.M. Fangio	51	T. Brooks	38	L. Villoresi	31
M. Hailwood	50	M. Gregory	38	W. von Trips	27
F. Cevert	47	G. Farina	33	S. Bellof	20
M. Hawthorn	45	A. Ascari	32	etc...	

Statistics - up to 31 December 1997 -

Number of laps led by driver (since 1957)

1	SENNA	2,999	Amongst current drivers:	
2	PROST	2,705		
3	MANSELL	2,099	VILLENEUVE	634
4	CLARK	2,039	COULTHARD	310
5	TEWART	1,893	ALESI	271
6	LAUDA	1,620	HAKKINEN	66
7	PIQUET	1,572	HERBERT	27
8	M. SCHUMACHER	1,568	PANIS	16
9	D. HILL	1,325	BARRICHELLO	8
10	G. HILL	1,073		
11	BRABHAM	827		

Number and percentage of podium finishes by current drivers

Example: Jacques Villeneuve has finished on the podium 19 times out of the 33 Grands Prix in which he has taken part. Therefore his percentage is 60.33%

1	J. VILLENEUVE	19/33	60.33%
2	D. HILL	46/84	54.57%
3	M. SCHUMACHER	62/10	51.27%
4	A. WURZ	1/3	33.33%
5	D. COULTHARD	15/58	25.91%
6	J. ALESI	31/135	22.96%
7	G. BERGER	48/210	22.85%
8	M. HAKKINEN	16/96	16.56%
9	H-H. FRENTZEN	8/65	12.30%
10	E. IRVINE	7/65	10.76%
11	G. FISICHELLA	2/25	8.00%
12	O. PANIS	5/59	7.11%
13	R. SCHUMACHER	1/17	5.89%
14	J. HERBERT	6/113	5.28%
15	J. VERSTAPPEN	2/48	4.16%
16	R. BARRICHELLO	2/81	2.46%

Number of fastest laps by a driver

PROST	41
MANSELL	30
CLARK	28
M. SCHUMACHER	28
FANGIO	23
PIQUET	23
BERGER	21
MOSS	20
SENNA	19
D. HILL	19
J. STEWART	15

Number of pole positions by a driver

SENNA	65	LAFFITE	7	ALESI	2
PROST	33	FITTIPALDI	6	LEWIS-EVANS	2
CLARK	33	P. HILL	6	SIFFERT	2
MANSELL	32	JABOUILLE	6	G.VILLENEUVE	2
FANGIO	28	JONES	6	WATSON	2
LAUDA	24	REUTEMANN	6	BANDINI	1
PIQUET	24	AMON	5	BARRICHELLO	1
D. HILL	20	COULTHARD	5	BONNIER	1
Ma. ANDRETTI	18	FARINA	5	BOUTSEN	1
ARNOUX	18	REGAZZONI	5	BRAMBILLA	1
STEWART	17	ROSBERG	5	CASTELLOTI	1
M. SCHUMACHER	17	TAMBAY	5	CESARIS	1
MOSS	16	HAWTHORN	4	COLLINS	1
ASCARI	14	PIRONI	4	DEPAILLER	1
HUNT	14	BROOKS	3	FRENTZEN	1
PETERSON	14	DE ANGELIS	3	GIACOMELLI	1
BRABHAM	13	T. FABI	3	HAKKINEN	1
G. HILL	13	GONZALES	3	HULME	1
ICKX	13	GURNEY	3	PACE	1
BERGER	12	JARIER	3	PARKES	1
RINDT	10	SCHECKTER	3	PRYCE	1
SURTEES	8	J.VILLENEUVE	3	REVSON	1
PATRESE	8	ALBORETO	2	VON TRIPS	1

Statistics - *(up to 31 December 1997)* -

Number of world championship titles by a driver

5 TITLES:
JUAN MANUEL FANGIO (ARGENTINA) 1951-54-55-56-57

4 TITLES:
ALAIN PROST (FRANCE) 1985-86-89-93

3 TITLES:
JACK BRABHAM	(AUSTRALIA)	1959-60-66
JACKIE STEWART	(GREAT BRITAIN)	1969-71-73
NIKI LAUDA	(AUSTRIA)	1975-77-84
NELSON PIQUET	(BRAZIL)	1981-83-87
AYRTON SENNA	(BRAZIL)	1988-90-91

2 TITLES:
ALBERTO ASCARI	(ITALY)	1952-53
GRAHAM HILL	(GREAT BRITAIN)	1962-68
JIM CLARK	(GREAT BRITAIN)	1963-65
EMERSON FITTIPALDI	(BRAZIL)	1972-74
MICHAEL SCHUMACHER	(GERMANY)	1994-95

1 TITLE:
GIUSEPPE FARINA	(ITALY)	1950
MIKE HAWTHORN	(GREAT BRITAIN)	1958
PHIL HILL	(UNITED STATES)	1961
JOHN SURTEES	(GREAT BRITAIN)	1964
DENIS HULME	(NEW ZEALAND)	1967
JOCHEN RINDT	(AUSTRIA)	1970
JAMES HUNT	(GREAT BRITAIN)	1976
MARIO ANDRETTI	(UNITED STATES)	1978
JODY SCHECKTER	(SOUTH AFRICA)	1979
ALAN JONES	(AUSTRALIA)	1980
KEKE ROSBERG	(FINLAND)	1982
NIGEL MANSELL	(GREAT BRITAIN)	1992
DAMON HILL	(GREAT BRITAIN)	1996
JACQUES VILLENEUVE	(CANADA)	1997

Number of kilometres in the lead by driver

The Brazilian Ayrton SENNA completed 13,613 kilometres in the lead. He heads Alain PROST (12,575) and Jim CLARK (10,189). Then, in descending order, MANSELL (9,642), STEWART (9,077), PIQUET (7,465), M. SCHUMACHER (7,211), LAUDA (7,188), D. HILL (6,062) and G. HILL (4,618) Although relatively new to F1, J. VILLENEUVE has already completed 2,972km at the head of the field

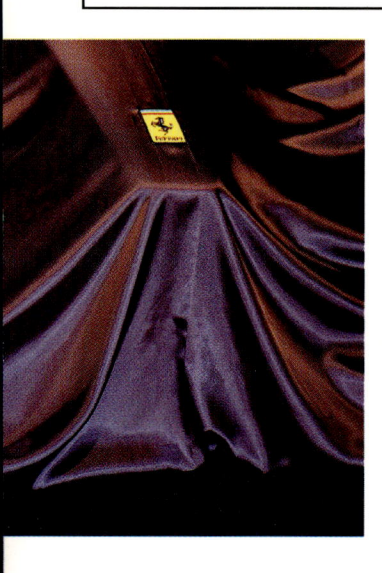

Number of Grand Prix victories by a driver

Driver	Wins	Driver	Wins
PROST	51	COULTHARD	2
SENNA	41	DE ANGELIS	2
MANSELL	31	DEPAILLER	2
STEWART	27	GONZALES	2
M. SCHUMACHER	27	HERBERT	2
CLARK	25	JABOUILLE	2
LAUDA	25	REVSON	2
FANGIO	24	RODRIGUEZ	2
PIQUET	23	SIFFERT	2
D. HILL	21	TAMBAY	2
MOSS	16	TRINTIGNANT	2
BRABHAM	14	VON TRIPS	2
FITTIPALDI	14	VUKOVICH	2
G. HILL	14	ALESI	1
ASCARI	13	BAGHETTI	1
Ma. ANDRETTI	12	BANDINI	1
JONES	12	BELTOISE	1
REUTEMANN	12	BONNIER	1
J. VILLENEUVE	11	BRAMBILLA	1
HUNT	10	BRYAN	1
PETERSON	10	CEVERT	1
SCHECKTER	10	FAGIOLI	1
BERGER	10	FLAHERTY	1
HULME	8	FRENTZEN	1
ICKX	8	GETHIN	1
ARNOUX	7	GINTHER	1
BROOKS	6	HAKKINEN	1
LAFFITE	6	HANKS	1
PATRESE	6	IRELAND	1
RINDT	6	MASS	1
SURTEES	6	MUSSO	1
G. VILLENEUVE	6	NANNINI	1
ALBORETO	5	NILSSON	1
FARINA	5	PACE	1
REGAZZONI	5	PANIS	1
ROSBERG	5	PARSONS	1
WATSON	5	RATHMAN	1
GURNEY	4	RUTTMAN	1
McLAREN	4	SCARFIOTTI	1
BOUTSEN	3	SWEIKERT	1
COLLINS	3	TARUFFI	1
P. HILL	3	WALLARD	1
PIRONI	3	WARD	1

NB: One should consider the fact that in 1950 the Formula One World Championship consisted of only 7 Grands Prix in the calendar year. As time went on the number of Grands Prix grew. Since 1984, there have been 16 per calendar year, and 17 in 1995 and 1997. Bearing this in mind, the greater the number of Grands Prix, the greater the chance to gain points, victories and new records.

Statistics - *up to 31 December 1997* -

Drivers with the most victories in a season

9 VICTOIRiES
- Nigel MANSELL in 1992 (WILLIAMS-RENAULT)
- Michael SCHUMACHER in 1995 (BENETTON-RENAULT)

8 VICTOIRiES
- Michael SCHUMACHER in 1994 (BENETTON-FORD)
- Ayrton SENNA in 1988 (McLAREN-HONDA)
- Damon HILL in 1996 (WILLIAMS-RENAULT)

7 VICTOIRiES
- Alain PROST in 1984 (McLAREN-PORSCHE)
- Alain PROST in 1988 (McLAREN-HONDA)
- Alain PROST in 1993 (WILLIAMS-RENAULT)
- Ayrton SENNA in 1991 (McLAREN-HONDA)
- Jim CLARK in 1963 (LOTUS-CLIMAX)
- Jacques VILLENEUVE in 1997 (WILLIAMS-RENAULT)

6 VICTOIRiES
- Jackie STEWART in 1969 and 1971 (MATRA-FORD and TYRRELL-FORD)
- Ayrton SENNA in 1989 and 1990 (McLAREN-HONDA)
- Alberto ASCARI in 1952 (FERRARI)
- Juan Manuel FANGIO in 1954 (MERCEDES and MASERATI)
- Jim CLARK in 1965 (LOTUS-CLIMAX)
- James HUNT in 1976 (McLAREN-FORD)
- Mario ANDRETTI in 1978 (LOTUS-FORD)
- Nigel MANSELL in 987 (WILLIAMS-HONDA)

5 VICTOIRiES
- Niki LAUDA in 1975,1976 (FERRARI) and 1984 (McLAREN-PORSCHE)
- Alain PROST in 1985 and 1990 (McLAREN PORSCHE and HONDA)
- Nigel MANSELL in 1986 and1991 (WILLIAMS-HONDA andt RENAULT)
- Alberto ASCARI in 1953 (FERRARI)
- Jack BRABHAM in 1960 (COOPER-CLIMAX)
- Jochen RINDT in 1970 (LOTUS-FORD)
- Emerson FITTIPALDI in 1972 (LOTUS-FORD)
- Jackie STEWART in 1973 (TYRRELL-FORD)
- Alan JONES in 1980 (WILLIAMS-FORD)
- Michael SCHUMACHER in 1997 (FERRARI)

Total number of points won by a driver

PROST	798.5	D. HILL	333	HERBERT	82
SENNA	614	REUTEMANN	310	FRENTZEN	71
PIQUET	485.5	G.HILL	289	J. VILLENEUVE	59
MANSELL	482	E. FITTIPALDI	281	PANIS	54
LAUDA	420.5	PATRESE	281	IRVINE	52
BERGER	385	FANGIO	277.5	BARRICHELLO	51
SCHUMACHER	362	CLARK	274	HAKKINEN	18
STEWART	360	COULTHARD	117	etc...	

Number of Grands Prix contested by a constructor

FERRARI	587		BENETTON	251
LOTUS	490		MINARDI	205
McLAREN	460		LOLA	139
TYRRELL	402		JORDAN	104
BRABHAM	394		SAUBER	81
WILLIAMS	379		PROST	17
LIGIER	326		STEWART	17
ARROWS	305			

Number of pole positions by a constructor

1	FERRARI	121	14	MERCEDES	8
2	LOTUS	107	15	VANWALL	7
3	WILLIAMS	107	16	MARCH	5
4	McLAREN	80	17	MATRA	4
5	BRABHAM	39	18	SHADOW	3
6	RENAULT	31	19	LANCIA	2
7	BENETTON	15	20	ARROWS	1
8	TYRRELL	14	21	HONDA	1
9	ALFA ROMEO	12	22	JORDAN	1
10	BRM	11	23	LOLA	1
11	COOPER	11	24	PORSCHE	1
12	MASERATI	10	25	WOLF	1
13	LIGIER	9			

Number of victories by a constructor

1	FERRARI	113	13	MASERATI	9
2	McLAREN	107	14	MATRA	9
3	WILLIAMS	103	15	MERCEDES	9
4	LOTUS	79	16	VANWALL	9
5	BRABHAM	35	17	MARCH	3
6	BENETTON	26	18	WOLF	3
7	TYRRELL	23	19	HONDA	2
8	BRM	17	20	HESKETH	1
9	COOPER	16	21	PENSKE	1
10	RENAULT	15	22	PORSCHE	1
11	ALFA ROMEO	10	23	SHADOW	1
12	LIGIER	9			

Statistics - up to 31 December 1997 -

Number of fastest laps by a constructor

FERRARI	126	ALFA ROMEO	14	SHADOW	2
WILLIAMS	109	COOPER	13	WOLF	2
LOTUS	71	MATRA	12	ENSIGN	1
McLAREN	69	LIGIER	11	GORDINI	1
BRABHAM	40	MERCEDES	9	HESKETH	1
BENETTON	36	MARCH	7	LANCIA	1
TYRRELL	20	VANWALL	6	PARNELLI	1
RENAULT	18	SURTEES	4	JORDAN	1
BRM	15	EAGLE	2		
MASERATI	15	HONDA	2		

Record number of points gained by a constructor in a season

1	McLAREN	199 points in 1988
2	WILLIAMS	175 points in 1996
3	WILLIAMS	168.5 points in 1993
4	WILLIAMS	164 points in 1992
5	McLAREN	143.5 points in 1984
6	McLAREN	141 points in 1989
7	WILLIAMS	141 points in 1986
8	BENETTON	137 points in 1995

etc.

NB: The World Championship scoring system has evolved over the years.

From 1950-1959 points were awarded 8-6-4-3-2 to the top five finishers, with a bonus point for fastest lap.
In 1960 the point for fastest lap was abolished and awarded instead to the sixth-placed finisher.
From 1961-1990 the race winner scored 9 points.
From 1991, in a bid to increase drivers' commitment, the prize for a race win rose to 10 points. For the other top five finishers the points remained the same. Constructors tally up the points scored by their cars. There have been rumours for a number of years that points will eventually be awarded to the top 10.

Number of pole positions by an engine

FORD	138
RENAULT	135
FERRARI	121
HONDA	74
CLIMAX	45
ALFA ROMEO	15
BMW	15
etc...	

Number of victories by an engine

FORD	174
FERRARI	113
RENAULT	95
HONDA	71
CLIMAX	40
PORSCHE	26
BRM	18
etc...	

Number of Grand Prix contested by an engine

FERRARI	587
FORD	451
RENAULT	284
ALFA ROMEO	212
BRM	197
HONDA	186
etc...	

Number of victories by a tyre manufacturer

GOODYEAR	361
DUNLOP	83
MICHELIN	59
FIRESTONE	49
PIRELLI	45
CONTINENTAL	10
ENGLEBERT	7

Constructors with the most Grand Prix victories in a season

McLAREN	15 victoiries in 1988
McLAREN	12 victoiries in 1984
WILLIAMS	12 victoiries in 1996
BENETTON	11 victoiries in 1995
WILLIAMS	10 victoiries in 1992 and 1993
McLAREN	10 victoiries in 1989
WILLIAMS	9 victoiries in 1986 and 1987

Number of constructors' World Championship titles

9 TITIES:
WILLIAMS 1980- 81 - 86 - 87 - 92 - 93 - 94 - 96 - 97

8 TITIES
FERRARI 1961 - 64 - 75 - 76 - 77 - 79 - 82 - 83

7 TITIES
LOTUS 1963 - 65 - 68 - 70 - 72 - 73 - 78
McLAREN 1974 - 84 - 85 - 88 - 89 - 90 - 91

2 TITIES
COOPER 1959 - 60
BRABHAM 1966 - 67

1 TITIE
VANWALL 1958
BRM 1962
MATRA 1969
TYRRELL 1971
BENETTON 1995

NB: The World Championship for constructors was only created in 1958

Final placings in the 1997 World Drivers' Championship

1	Jacques VILLENEUVE	81 points
2	Heinz-Harald FRENTZEN	42
3	David COULTHARD	36
4	Jean ALESI	36
5	Gerhard BERGER	27
6	Mika HAKKINEN	27
7	Eddie IRVINE	24
8	Giancarlo FISICHELLA	20
9	Olivier PANIS	16
10	Johnny HERBERT	15
11	Ralf SCHUMACHER	13
12	Damon HILL	7
13	Rubens BARRICHELLO	6
14	Alexander WURZ	4
15	Jarno TRULLI	3
16	Mika SALO	2
17	Pedro DINIZ	2
18	Shinji NAKANO	2
19	Nicola LARINI	1

NB: On November 11 Michael Schumacher (78 points) was excluded from second place in the 1997 world championship as a consequence of his collision with Jacques Villeneuve at Jerez on 26 October. Despite this penalty, his five race wins still count towards his career record.

Greatest number of pole positions in a season by a driver

N. MANSELL	14 in 1992	(WILLIAMS-RENAULT)
A. PROST	13 in 1993	(WILLIAMS-RENAULT)
A. SENNA	13 in 1988	(McLAREN-HONDA)
A. SENNA	13 in 1989	(McLAREN-HONDA)
A. SENNA	10 in 1990	(McLAREN-HONDA)
J. VILLENEUVE	10 in 1997	(WILLIAMS-RENAULT)
R. PETERSON	9 in 1973	(LOTUS-FORD)
N. LAUDA	9 in 1974	(FERRARI)
N. LAUDA	9 in 1975	(FERRARI)
N. PIQUET	9 in 1984	(BRABHAM-FORD)
D. HILL	9 in 1996	(WILLIAMS-RENAULT)
A. SENNA	8 in 1986	(LOTUS-RENAULT)
A. SENNA	8 in 1991	(McLAREN-HONDA)
J. HUNT	8 in 1976	(McLAREN-FORD)
M. ANDRETTI	8 in 1978	(LOTUS-FORD)
N. MANSELL	8 in 1987	(WILLIAMS-HONDA)

etc...

The Brazilian Ayrton SENNA holds the record for the number of consecutive pole positions. He claimed 8 poles between the 1988 Spanish Grand Prix and the 1989 American Grand Prix.

Constructors with the greatest number of pole positions in a season

McLAREN	15 pole positions in 1988 and 1989
WILLIAMS	15 pole positions in 1992 and 1993
LOTUS	12 pole positions in 1978
WILLIAMS	12 pole positions in 1987, 1995 and 1996
McLAREN	12 pole positions in 1990
WILLIAMS	11 pole positions in 1997
LOTUS	10 pole positions in 1973
FERRARI	10 pole positions in 1974

The WILLIAMS team monopolised pole position between the 1992 French Grand Prix and the 1993 Japanese Grand Prix (a total of 24 races) - a Grand Prix record. WILLIAMS are also the only team to have held pole position throughout an entire Grand Prix season, in 1993.

Final placings in the 1997 World Constructors' Championship

1	Williams-Renault	123 points
2	Ferrari	102
3	Benetton-Renault	67
4	McLaren-Mercedes	63
5	Jordan-Peugeot	33
6	Prost-Mugen-Honda	21
7	Sauber-Petronas	16
8	Arrows-Yamaha	9
9	Stewart-Ford	6
10	Tyrrell-Ford	2

Achevé d'imprimer
sur les presses de l'imprimerie **S**ézanne
Dépôt légal
Avril 1998